"Who did God make me to be? is seldom asked. V
nesses, and inabilities. And even when the questio:
wisdom. *Rhythms for Life* by Alastair Sterne is a happy exception. It a̶s̶s̶e̶r̶t̶s̶ ̶
reality of who each of us is uniquely created to be and then gives a grace-filled path to
get there."

Todd Hunter, bishop in the Anglican Church in North America, author of *Christianity Beyond Belief*

"At once deeply personal and immensely practical, Alastair has written a powerful book
that can change the way we move through the world. He inspires us to cultivate
rhythms that enable us to experience deep contentment, joy, and peace in our everyday
life with God."

Ken Shigematsu, pastor of Tenth Church, Vancouver, British Columbia, and author of *Survival Guide for the Soul*

"As people on a faith journey, an essential ingredient to our continued development is
the ability to take the intangible and make it tangible, to make the foreign and unfamiliar personal and intimate. This book provides an invitation for the intangible,
foreign, perhaps vast and unfamiliar aspects of faith to have invitations in the daily, the
present, and the very much 'right here' of our lives. I'm grateful that this book exists
to help us know and experience what is always true: that God loves us and can be found
right here in the rhythms of life."

Hillary McBride, therapist, author, and podcaster

"I've known Alastair Sterne for over a decade now. From our initial introduction in one
of my courses, he stood out as a deeply formed and committed disciple of Jesus. We connected over our shared interest in church planting and missional engagement. This book
shows the 'secret sauce' that allows Alastair to remain a deeply formed and committed
disciple of Jesus. Better yet, he points the way for all of us. *Rhythms for Life* is not simply
another book on spiritual formation. There are plenty of those. This is a field manual
that all God's people can follow to set themselves up for long-term growth in God's grace.
Alastair writes with theological and biblical depth in a fully accessible manner for our
post-Christendom contexts. He begins with the critical need to uncover our true identity
in Christ and then moves to the crafting of a personal rule of life. I found the worksheets
and exercises to flow seamlessly from the teaching and to be profoundly enriching. In
short, Alastair introduces the great tradition of spiritual formation for a new generation.
I hope this book becomes a classic with a long shelf life. I know that my soul has been
warmed anew while reading this and working through the exercises."

Brian Russell, professor, associate provost, and dean of the Asbury Theological Seminary
Orlando School of Ministry

"There is only one you. God's creative design template for your life includes rhythms
and relationships that express the true you in the context of your community. Alastair
Sterne gently encourages his readers to pay attention to God's unique thumbprint
graced upon them and embody it abundantly."

Stephen A. Macchia, founder and president of Leadership Transformations, author of *Crafting a Rule of Life*

"In virtually every area of life, the condition of flourishing is supported by an unwavering commitment to practices. Flourishing athletes work out and eat well, flourishing musicians repeat their scales, flourishing students abide by rigorous study schedules, and flourishing family members engage attentively, to name a few. Likewise, the flourishing that comes from being formed into the likeness of Jesus Christ doesn't just happen to us as we sit passively 'letting go and letting God.' Rather, it happens as we respond to God through active participation in long-standing, proven practices that support the flourishing of our entire selves. In *Rhythms for Life*, Alastair Sterne has provided an excellent road map for this very purpose."

Scott Sauls, senior pastor of Christ Presbyterian Church in Nashville, Tennessee, and author of *Jesus Outside the Lines*

"*Rhythms for Life* is a practical guide to spiritual formation *within* Christian community *for* missional engagement where you live, right now. And it's written by a pastor who understands how people work and how the Holy Spirit changes hearts. Work through this book with friends or family—or your whole congregation—and you will be enriched."

Brandon J. O'Brien, director of content development and distribution for Redeemer City to City

"All theology should be applied theology, at least that was the argument of one of the best teachers I know, and the insight is ancient. As Jesus said to Nicodemus, the teacher of Israel, 'The reason you don't understand is that you don't do the truth.' That disconnect is a perennial problem, even when we yearn for more integrity. Alastair Sterne has written a book for all of us, but specially so for those who want to understand the integral relationship of what they believe with the way that they live. In *Rhythms for Life* he has woven together theology and experience with a rare wisdom born of his years of loving people who long for more flourishing in their lives for the sake of their cities."

Steven Garber, author of *The Seamless Life* and professor of marketplace theology at Regent College

"A big part of following Jesus is knowing who you are and how he created you to be, so you can use your unique gifts to glorify his kingdom. This book will guide you through the process of discerning just that and establishing rhythms to live out your vocation. It is a must-read for any season and rhythm of life."

Albert Tate, cofounder and lead pastor of Fellowship Church, Monrovia, California

"It seems to me that the healthiest Christians are the most ordinary people—but they did not arrive there by accident. They have had the painstaking struggle of knowing themselves, being faithful in the small things, not ignoring the gifts of their community, appreciating the discipline of Scripture, and . . . *voila!* An ordinary, faithful Christian. God give us more of them! Thankfully Alastair provides a clear path for churches who desire to be a breeding ground for Christians like this."

Julie Canlis, lecturer for Whitworth's graduate studies in theology program, author of *Calvin's Ladder* and *A Theology of the Ordinary*

Rhythms for LIFE

Spiritual Practices for Who God Made You to Be

Alastair Sterne

An imprint of InterVarsity Press
Downers Grove, Illinois

InterVarsity Press
P.O. Box 1400, Downers Grove, IL 60515-1426
ivpress.com
email@ivpress.com

InterVarsity Press® is the book-publishing division of InterVarsity Christian Fellowship/USA®, a movement of students and faculty active on campus at hundreds of universities, colleges, and schools of nursing in the United States of America, and a member movement of the International Fellowship of Evangelical Students. For information about local and regional activities, visit intervarsity.org.

All Scripture quotations, unless otherwise indicated, are taken from The Holy Bible, New International Version®, NIV®. Copyright © 1973, 1978, 1984, 2011 by Biblica, Inc.™ Used by permission of Zondervan. All rights reserved worldwide. www.zondervan.com. The "NIV" and "New International Version" are trademarks registered in the United States Patent and Trademark Office by Biblica, Inc.™

While any stories in this book are true, some names and identifying information may have been changed to protect the privacy of individuals.

Cover design and image composite: David Fassett
Interior design: Jeanna Wiggins
Images: maze with person: © CSA Images / Getty Images
         man standing on shore: © Jarmo Piironen / iStock / Getty Images Plus
         postage stamp border: © troyek / E+ / Getty Images

ISBN 978-0-8308-3197-5 (print)
ISBN 978-0-8308-3198-2 (digital)

Printed in the United States of America ∞

InterVarsity Press is committed to ecological stewardship and to the conservation of natural resources in all our operations. This book was printed using sustainably sourced paper.

Library of Congress Cataloging-in-Publication Data
A catalog record for this book is available from the Library of Congress.

P 25 24 23 22 21 20 19 18 17 16 15 14 13 12 11 10 9 8 7 6 5 4 3 2 1
Y 41 40 39 38 37 36 35 34 33 32 31 30 29 28 27 26 25 24 23 22 21 20

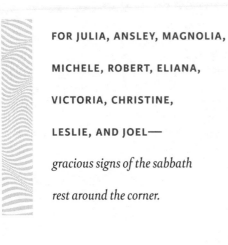

FOR JULIA, ANSLEY, MAGNOLIA,

MICHELE, ROBERT, ELIANA,

VICTORIA, CHRISTINE,

LESLIE, AND JOEL—

gracious signs of the sabbath

rest around the corner.

Contents

Introduction

Rhythms for the Journey

[God] called you through our gospel, so that you may
obtain the glory of our Lord Jesus Christ.

2 THESSALONIANS 2:14

If seeds in the black earth can turn into such beautiful roses, what might
not the heart of man become in its long journey toward the stars?

G. K. CHESTERTON

I GREW UP ON VANCOUVER ISLAND in the Pacific Northwest. Once my friends and I had driver's licenses, it wasn't uncommon for us to get in the car and drive aimlessly within the confines of our island and the amount of gas we could afford.

We usually didn't get very far.

But the destination wasn't the point.

Our drives were about our enjoyment of each other. The forests lining the contours of mountains and the smell of the ocean served as the backdrop. We drove with the windows down and the music loud, and sang our favorite songs as our sides ached from laughter.

But most journeys require more structure. Especially if they ask for more commitment than a half day. Before we set off on a bigger adventure, at least two questions need to be answered:

- Where are we going?

- And how are we going to get there?

Jesus invites us on a journey. Two disruptive words alter the course of our lives: "Follow me." Fishermen lay down their nets. Tax collectors leave their booths. Revolutionaries lay down their arms. And countless people throughout the millennia have reordered their lives around the gospel.

We go wherever Jesus goes.

The invitation doesn't come with a road map laying out the specifics of how the rest of our lives will go, however. But that's okay. What matters most on the journey is that we go with him. Because as we get our feet dusty on the path, we walk with none other than God himself. No wonder Frederick Buechner put it like this: "I think of my life and the lives of everyone who has ever lived, or ever will live, as not just journeys through time but as sacred journeys."[1] Much like the excursions of my youth, the journey with Jesus is full of wonder and joy. Because this is the most sacred path we can tread. He has pioneered and opened up the only path to life with God.

Christlikeness

When G. K. Chesterton reflected on the Christian faith, he described it as a breathtaking "journey toward the stars."[2] And like any grand adventure, you will not be the same person you were when you left. Each and every step with Jesus changes us along the way.

This is a transformative journey.

The writers of Scripture tell us that, on the way, we become "participa[nts] in the divine nature" (2 Pet 1:3-4), and are "being transformed into his image with ever-increasing glory" (2 Cor 3:18) until we "share in the glory of our Lord Jesus Christ" (2 Thess 2:14). If we follow Jesus, we become like him, which is traditionally called Christlikeness.

But what is Christlikeness?

Christlikeness is your reflection of Jesus. You become present to the presence of Jesus in every area of your life. And you contribute to the reflection of his character within the life of your community.

Christlikeness includes imitating Jesus as our model. But it goes beyond that. A child might initially develop as an artist by copying images with tracing paper. At first the copies will be obvious. But over time, they might create convincing copies. Eventually they can leave the tracing paper on the shelf because the practice of imitation developed actual skill and true artistry.

As we pursue Jesus, we take out the tracing paper and, line by line, try to copy him in our lives. But God is not content with mere copies. The apostle Paul describes us as God's "handiwork," which can be translated as his "masterpiece" or even "poem" (Eph 2:10). God transforms us from mere copyists into the artistry of Christ. Because God isn't interested in minor adjustments. God the Father has our full transformation in mind. Nothing less than the very best version of ourselves—alive and flourishing in Christ.

But how are we going to get there?

Take a breath. Instill this in your heart:

God does not expect us to do this on our own.

It does not rest entirely on our shoulders.

Christlikeness for us is Christ in us.

The gospel is the good news about everything Jesus has accomplished to save us and all of creation. Everything Jesus has done for us was so that we could be "in him."[3] We get to share in the very life of God. Jesus lives in us and makes us one with him—much like a husband and wife become one (see Jn 17:20-23; 1 Cor 6:17; and Gal 2:20). Our growth in Christlikeness is as simple as spending time with Jesus. We see the glory of God in the face of Christ (2 Cor 4:6). And as we do so, we are steadily transformed into his likeness. It doesn't depend on our strength. The Spirit is at work in us (2 Cor 3:18). Christlikeness is a gift we receive.

The pressure is off.

Rhythm for Life

The Spirit assures our transformation, yet we do not become Christlike by accident. We can't drift into it. It requires intentionality on our part as we "work out [our] salvation" in response to what God initiates in us (Phil 2:12-13). As Dallas Willard—a philosopher and the author of many books on spiritual formation—helpfully says, "The path of spiritual growth in the riches of Christ is not a passive one. Grace is not opposed to effort. It is opposed to earning. Effort is action. Earning is attitude."[4] Grace empowers us to put in intentional effort without falling into the unmanageable pressure and unattainable goal of earning God's approval or love.

Even though we are not handed a road map for this journey with Jesus, we can still create some guidelines to help us stay on course. I have found that a plan for growing in Christlikeness helps. And I am hardly the first to make this discovery.

Originating in the monastic tradition in the fifth century, the practice of living by a rule of life has sustained Christians throughout the ages. Essentially, in a rule of life you identify habits, disciplines, and practices to keep you moving in the direction of Jesus with your community. We have Saint Benedict of Nursia to thank for his contribution to this practice. Benedict taught that a rule of life was not meant to be burdensome but could help us remain in "the ineffable sweetness of love."[5] Intentionality sounds pretty good when you put it like that.

The practice of crafting a rule of life is hardly exclusive to the monastic life. For example, the Book of Common Prayer (BCP) from the Anglican tradition suggests, "Every Christian man or woman should from time to time frame for themselves a Rule of Life in accordance with the precepts of the Gospel and the faith and order of the Church."[6] Benedict created a communal rule. The BCP invites us to create a personal rule—personal, that is, but not individualistic. It can help anchor us to the gospel and to the shared practices of our community

Yet I prefer the language of "rhythm for life" over "rule of life."

Life moves along with seasons of rigidity, flexibility, spontaneity, and discipline. What works for six months may not work for the next six months. Life is dynamic, not static. As the BCP suggests, we should sometimes revise our plans for spiritual formation. The word *rhythm* reminds us that life changes. We need to assess our habits and practices in light of our phase of life and to wrestle with what is best for us at our particular moment in time. There are seasons for everything under the sun.

My own rhythm for life has changed multiple times. It changed drastically when my children were born. As a new parent, it became much harder to carve out the same amount of time in the morning and evening for Scripture, prayer, and journaling, let alone the same amount of undistracted quality time. I barely had any contemplative capacity. When I tried to sit quietly with Jesus, I fell asleep. Initially I tried to double down and make my routine work. But it didn't work. And I fell into the mistake of feeling "far" from God solely because of my slipping discipline. But God's presence isn't contingent on my performance. Instead of lingering in guilt, I sought to discover new expressions of practices for that sleepless season. As my children have moved out of the "destroy any resemblance of adequate sleep for mommy and daddy" stage, my practices have changed again.

A few years ago, I experienced a prolonged season of depression. Once again, my practices changed. Part of my recovery involved discovering new practices of self-care, such as running and medicine, along with renewed disciplines of gratitude and encouragement. Although my depression made it hard to feel "close" to God, saying thank you for something as basic as a warm home helped me remember that all of life is grace. I also pressed into a vision bigger than the here and now, which kindled my hope in a difficult time.

Because of how life unfolds and changes, our spiritual practices need to be dynamic. This means a rhythm for life is always open to revision. It isn't set in stone. And it's never a measure of our success or failure in spiritual growth. If we treat it this way we can become prideful based on our performance or crushed by shame because we aren't living up to our ideals. But there's no need to perform or evaluate ourselves in this way. We are accepted and loved by Jesus. A rhythm for life is simply a way to bring intentionality into our pursuit of him.

Becoming Who God Made You to Be

I wrote this book to help you grow in Christlikeness by crafting your own rhythm for life. It is not a self-help book. Rather, I want to tune you into your call to follow Jesus. This is called *vocation*. I define *vocation* as your identity uniquely lived out before God. The goal is to develop a rhythm for life in response to your God-given vocation.

Although there are many common elements in people's rhythms for life, there is no generic template for growing in Christlikeness. There is no one-size-fits-all approach. Who you are matters. You are a significant factor in your plan for spiritual formation.

I write as a pastor. I draw from my experience in walking people through this process. But I also write out of my own struggle to make sense of my life. It took me years to embrace my uniqueness as an indispensable part of my journey with God. As I have learned to accept my whole self before God, my approach to spiritual practices has changed. I have found expressions of common practices that resonate more readily with who God made me to be. And I continue to discover how each habit and discipline can help me connect with God and my vocation.

This book contains two parts. Part one, "Discerning Who God Has Made You to Be," is composed of five chapters. These chapters are designed for you to reflect on who God has made you to be. In the first chapter, you'll consider your identity. In the second, you'll discern your spiritual gifts and talents and examine how your personality shapes your use of them. In the third chapter, you'll identify your values and virtues and how they are aligned or misaligned with the kingdom of God. In the fourth, you'll reflect on your roles in life and the way each role can reflect the image of God. In the last chapter of part one, you'll learn about vocation and craft a personal vocation statement. These chapters and exercises are meant to be brief, not exhaustive, and they work together as a blueprint for part two.

In the second part, "Rhythms for Living Your Vocation," you will work through the four rhythms for life: up, in, with, and out. Each chapter will help you identify practices that keep you moving upward to God, inward to self, withward in community, and outward in mission. These four chapters also help you identify expressions of practices that root you in these rhythms.

The end result of this book is a rhythm for life. But your rhythm itself will not assure your transformation. My hope for you is that a rhythm for life will encourage you to depend on the work of the Spirit in your life to empower your growth (2 Thess 2:13).

I have two encouragements as you begin. First, please pace yourself. Do not try to consume this book quickly. Our formation takes time. You will be better off if you slowly work through each chapter, perhaps spending a week or even two on each one. Don't skip past the worksheets either. Prayerfully engage with and reflect on them. If you're typically in a hurry, you may want to read the epilogue first. This book is set at the pace of Godspeed.

Second, please work through this book with others. On this journey, you not only need to know your destination; you also need to know your traveling companions. We can't become fully like Jesus in isolated bubbles. We're children in the midst of a new family. The Spirit dwells in the divine "y'all." As the apostle Paul writes, "Do you not know that you yourselves [plural] are God's temple and that God's Spirit dwells in your [plural] midst?" (1 Cor 3:16). God calls us to journey together.

If you haven't already, I encourage you to reach out to a few trusted friends or your wider church community and ask them to go through this with you. I hope the content and exercises will ignite an ongoing process of exploration and conversation between you and your community of faith. There is a framework in "Crafting Your Rhythms for Life in Community," appendix A, for working through the book with others. But right now, why don't you take a moment to pray and consider who you'd like to invite on this journey with you?

Who are the people you'll work through this book with?

_____

_____

_____

_____

The invitation to follow Jesus is a journey. We go wherever Jesus goes. Let's intentionally move in his direction, one step at a time.

Part One

Discerning Who God Has Made You to Be

1

Identity

God created mankind in his own image,
in the image of God he created them;
male and female he created them.

GENESIS 1:27

Quit keeping score altogether and surrender yourself with
all your sinfulness to God who sees neither the score nor the
scorekeeper but only his child redeemed by Christ.

THOMAS MERTON

MY FIRST EXISTENTIAL CRISIS HAPPENED when I was fourteen (you can decide whether I was early or late to the game). In my bedroom I stepped in front of the full-length mirror on my closet door. My hair was dyed. I was wearing a gaudy industrial-band shirt. Nothing out of the ordinary. But as I stood and gazed at myself, something shifted. I became aware of how I was looking back at myself. I thought: *I exist.*

I wasn't about to win any philosophical awards. But I was conscious of the realness of myself in a new way. It unnerved me. Because I also wondered: *Who am I?*

I thought of my name, my family, and my short history. I ran through my interests, friends, and dreams. They all contributed to who I am. But these facts didn't answer the question. At least not in a way that settled me. I tried to go on with my day. But the thought followed me the way fruit flies gravitate to overripe oranges. I couldn't swat it away.

Who am I?

This question is often on our minds or close by. You may have only begun to search for an answer. If you recently entered a new season, you may be asking, *Who will I become?* Or, if a transition or crisis has made you feel as if part of yourself has been lost, you might be wondering, *Who am I now?* It's possible to search your soul and yet not be convinced by what you've found. And whether we have a satisfying answer or not, we never stop asking the question. It's essential.

But how we ask the question affects the quality of the answer. We can learn to ask it well. After years of searching, I discovered the best form is, *Whose am I?* Because whether our life stories are written in pen, sketched in pencil, or painted on a canvas, questions of identity are about authorship. Who writes your story?

Misguided Stories

Many stories guide our lives. But often our stories are misguided. We can find ourselves in undesirable story lines and plot twists. Before we can untangle ourselves from misguided stories, we need to name them—and identify their authors.

One dominant story of modern Western culture is that we are our own, the authors of our fate. "No one has the right to define who you are except you; you write your own story," or so the story goes. We're encouraged to claim our self-authorship. But identity isn't this simple.

We exist within the world. We determine who we are to some extent, but we are not exempt from outside influences. Countless people shape us. Friends, family, teachers, and coworkers, to name a few. The idea of self-authorship is appealing because it keeps us at the center of the story. But it's not the whole story. There are others who wrote the script first, before we put our name on it. We are co-authors at best.

Another common story is the performance story. If you grew up in a family or culture where performance and achievements are highly regarded, you may have internalized a story that says you are only valuable if you excel and accomplish many things with your life.

Imagine a father who drives his son to school in a luxury car. As his son grabs his backpack and scoots out of the car, the father says without fail, "Be exceptional." The tone is always positive. He intends to encourage his son. As days accumulate into years, his son internalizes this message. But what is the story?

This is a performance story. The father wants more than a son who does well in life. He wants his child to be better than the rest. He wants him to stand tall above his peers. And while the story has the capacity to motivate the son to accomplish great things, it also has the strength to crush his self-worth. What happens if he isn't exceptional? Or when he realizes there is someone more exceptional than him? Or if he fails? Even if these negative effects were never the father's intent, he wrote a performance story for his son.

Unfortunately, the reality is that stories can be harmful and can even contaminate. People who have been emotionally or physically traumatized often internalize a story that says they are worthless. They can even believe that they deserved what happened. These kinds of contamination stories can motivate people to prove their worth and do many good things throughout their life. But contamination stories can also have the opposite effect. Sometimes people hold back and play it safe because failure would validate the message of their misguided story: they are worthless. Contamination stories wreak havoc in our lives because they tell us we are not enough and never will be.[1]

We allow many stories to guide and direct our lives. We inherit them from our family and friends. We are taught them through education, popular culture, and entertainment. Whatever the source, many of our stories are hopelessly misguided. But all of them try to answer the question, "Who am I?"

Two dominant stories shaped my identity.

The first I call "almost but not enough." I started living by this story after I was dumped for the first time at sixteen. I thought I had found everlasting love. But it wasn't mutual. I felt something was wrong with me. "Almost but not enough." Over the years I overcompensated for the "almost but not enough" narrative by motivating myself with different stories, such as, "Be the best. Do something impressive." This is nothing short of a performance story. It's how I learned to compensate.

The second I call "exciting but wrong." Through experiences in my childhood I learned to push boundaries. I internalized a story that said the best sources of excitement are usually wrong. It started with "innocent" wrongs: stealing garden gnomes or sneaking out at night. But as I grew up, "exciting but wrong" translated into an unbounded sexual life, experimentation with many drugs, unfaithfulness in intimate relationships, and pushing healthy boundaries in friendships. This is a contamination story.

Both of my misguided stories created toxic shame in my life. I developed a deeply held belief that something was wrong with me. I knew I wasn't enough. As a result, I was never sure who I was. It has taken years to disentangle from these stories. And I still tell them to myself occasionally. Sometimes they just start to play in my mind. But these misguided stories have progressively lost their influence and strength as I've answered the better question, "Whose am I?"

Our True Story

The apostle Paul had a countercultural message for the church in Corinth. It continues to challenge our own assumptions about identity. He wrote, "You are not your own; you were bought at a price" (1 Cor 6:19-20).

We belong to Christ.

This is the good news of the gospel.

Jesus Christ has written a story of redemption for the world and continues to write his story within each of us. He disentangles us from our misguided stories as we accept his invitation to follow him into the true story of God.[2] Under God's authorship we find our creational identity, our redemptive identity, and adoption.

Creational identity. The story of the Bible begins with the book of Genesis, which tells us something fundamental about all people: we are made in the image of God (Gen 1:26-27). This is our creational identity.

Imagine a mirror set at a forty-five-degree angle. If you shine light directly on it from above it will reflect horizontally out into the room. In the same way, we can imagine ourselves as mirrors. God shines on us to be reflected through us into the world. We were created to reflect the image of our triune God.

One of the greatest mysteries of faith is the Trinity.

God is one God in three persons. God the Father, the Son, and the Holy Spirit. Three persons in one nature.[3] The apostle John wrote in one of his letters, "God is love" (1 Jn 4:8). The church father Saint Augustine helped us try to wrap our minds around this mystery when he said that God is at once lover, beloved, and love itself. Neither Augustine nor John intended to reduce God to the emotion of love. Instead, their words point to how love dances back and forth between the three persons of the Trinity. This is why we can say that God *is* love.

This means that in eternity past, God wasn't singing, "Can anybody find me somebody to love?"[4] God created us out of the abundance and overflow of his love and not out of loneliness or neediness. He created us to be loved by him and to love him.

Since we are made in God's image, we are also created to love and be loved by others. You may have heard or sung worship songs with lyrics such as, "You're all I need, God." This isn't the whole picture. In the Garden, God said to Adam, "It is not good for the man to be alone" (Gen 2:18). We are only fully human when God's love flows back and forth between us and other people as well.

When we turn to God as the author of our story, we discover our creational identity: we were made in the image of God. We receive and reflect his love. We were made to do so in relationship. God has written our story not with pencil, ink, or paint but with love.

But our creational identity is only one part of the first chapter of the story.

The story written by God isn't always comfortable for us because love includes truth. God is a loving truth-speaker. As theologian and ethicist Stanley Hauerwas writes, "The story Christians tell of God exposes the unwelcome fact that I am a sinner. For without such a narrative the fact and nature of my sin cannot help but remain hidden in self-deception."[5] The story of God graciously brings us out of hiding and into an honest assessment of ourselves before God: our creational identity has fallen and shattered, like a mirror broken into shards of glass.

The myth of self-authorship began long before our era. Genesis 3 recalls how sin entered the world. Adam and Eve deliberately rejected God's goodness, trustworthiness, and authorship and gave in to the temptation to write their own life stories apart from God's presence and authority. They broke his simple instruction so they could "be like God, knowing good and evil" despite already being image bearers (Gen 3:5). The apostle Paul wrote to the Romans that, with this act, "sin entered the world through one man, and death through sin, and in this way death came to all people, because all sinned" (Rom 5:12).[6]

But what happened in the Garden has happened in every single one of our lives as well.

Sometimes we make sin too small by reducing it to breaking rules. But as New Testament scholar William Barclay writes, "Sin is a crime, not [only] against law, but against love."[7] Sin isn't just breaking rules; it's infidelity and unfaithfulness. When a spouse cheats in marriage, yes, they are breaking a vow in the covenant of marriage. They are breaking a rule. But more fundamentally they are sinning against the love that was supposed to unite and sustain them in marriage. In other words, the sin is expressed in the breaking of a vow, but its weightiness is due to the relationship that is broken. In a similar way, Adam and Eve broke the one commandment in the Garden. But the reason their action was so severe and weighty was because they deliberately rejected God's loving union with them. They sinned not only against law but also against love.

The consequence of original sin was that the image of God in us was damaged, distorted, and corrupted. We were made to dwell and rejoice in God's love and to reflect his love into all of creation. But humanity has been alienated and separated from God's loving presence. And our spiritual condition has led to brokenness, disorder, pollution, and all kinds of evil in the world. Sin has corrupted us to the core. This truth led the Reformer John Calvin to write, "Although some obscure lineaments of that image are found remaining in us; yet [they are] so vitiated and maimed, that they may truly be said to be destroyed."[8] Our creational identity has been so badly damaged by our sin that it is beyond our own recovery. Our creational identity needs to be rescued and restored.

Redemptive identity. We must look at how God's story culminates in Jesus to discover our redemptive identity. Luke reported in his Gospel that when angels appeared to the shepherds to lead them toward the newborn Christ, one angel declared, "Do not be afraid. I bring you good news that will cause great joy for all the people" (Lk 2:10). Why was this news so good and joyful? The angel continued, "Today in the town of David a Savior has been born to you;

he is the Messiah, the Lord" (Lk 2:11). The gospel is good news, not good advice. It is the declaration about Jesus Christ and all that he has done to fulfill God's story for the sake of the world as our Savior and Redeemer.

There are a lot of theories about who Jesus was: a good man, a teacher, a mistaken end-times prophet, an exaggeration of his disciples' imagination, or even nonexistent. A distinctly different answer is given by the writers of Scripture. One of the simplest answers is that Jesus is Immanuel, which means "God with us" (see Mt 1:23). Jesus of Nazareth, the Son of God, entered the world and became one of us. The incarnation cozies up with the Trinity as another great mystery. Jesus is both God and man, perfectly divine and perfectly human.

But why did he come into the world and take on our form? I find that it's best to take Jesus at his own word: he came to be rejected, crucified, buried, and raised from the dead.[9] He came not for the healthy but the sick. He didn't come for those who have their act together but for sinners (Mk 2:17). The one who made the heavens and the earth dragged a tree that he made (and that humanity fashioned into a cross) through the dirt of the earth, and there he was crucified. He died on two crooked beams in ancient Rome, not by accident, but according to plan.

What could possibly motivate Jesus to do this?

What motivated God to create us in the first place?

Love.

The apostle Paul wrote to the church in Ephesus, "Because of his great love for us, God, who is rich in mercy, made us alive with Christ even when we were dead in transgressions" (Eph 2:4-5). God didn't send Jesus into the world *so that* he could love us. God sent Jesus into the world *because* he always has loved us. We must not get our wires crossed on this point. Jesus died for us as a revelation of God's profound love for us.

Love came for us even when we least deserved it. This is a non-negotiable truth: our sins required a cross. The joy of bringing us back home motivated Jesus to endure the worst fate (Heb 12:2). Jesus took on our sins in his body and faced the consequences on our behalf. On the cross, he uttered a cry we will never comprehend nor say ourselves: "My God, my God, why have you forsaken me?" (Mt 27:46; Mk 15:34). And he did it all out of love.

When Peter, one of Jesus' closest friends and an apostle, tried to comprehend what took place on the cross, he concluded, "[Jesus] himself bore our sins in his body on the cross so that we might die to sins and live for righteousness. By his wounds you have been healed" (1 Pet 2:24). Similarly, author and pastor Tim Keller writes, "We are more sinful and flawed in ourselves than we ever dared believe, yet at the very same time we are more loved and accepted in Jesus Christ than we ever dared hope."[10]

Through his death and resurrection, Jesus forgives our sins and washes them away, overcomes death with eternal life, reconciles us into a loving relationship with God, restores the image of God within us, assures us of our future in his kingdom, and empowers new life that starts now. This is the great story of redemption written by Jesus Christ.

But what does it mean for who we are?

Adoption. When we place our faith in Jesus, we are no longer our own: we belong to Christ (Rom 8:9). We are adopted into the family of God as beloved children (Rom 8:15; Eph 1:4-6; Gal 4:4-5). The Spirit of God fills us so that the cry of our hearts becomes, "Abba! Father!" (Rom 8:12-17; Gal 4:6-7). The great theologian J. I. Packer is convinced that adoption is the highest privilege the gospel offers. He writes, "In adoption, God takes us into his family and fellowship—he establishes us as his children and heirs. Closeness, affection and generosity are at the heart of the relationship. To be right with God the Judge [justification] is a great thing, but to be loved and cared for by God the Father [adoption] is a greater thing."[11]

What is the implication of our adoption?

We don't have to be hindered by our misguided stories. We don't need to define ourselves, or perform, or remain contaminated. This profound gift of grace led Thomas Merton to write, "Quit keeping score altogether and surrender yourself with all your sinfulness to God who sees neither the score nor the scorekeeper but only his child redeemed by Christ."[12] We are free to enjoy God and delight in his love for endless days. We don't merely bide our time, waiting with bated breath until the kingdom arrives in its fullness. Because our lives with Christ start now and not just later.

There's nothing we have to do to be loved by God; we simply receive what he offers in abundance through Christ our Redeemer. We are loved because we are loved. We have always been loved and always will be loved. Nothing can separate us from the love of God in Christ Jesus (Rom 8:38-39). This is what makes the journey of following Christ such a great joy, even through the shadows and darkness cast by the trials and suffering we'll face.

Although our creational identity was vandalized by sin, it is now restored and healed through our redemptive identity. The two go hand in hand. We are image bearers of God, made to be loved and to love, to live in relationship and community, as God's beloved children. This is the identity God has for you. This is how he defines you. This is who you are in Christ.

Between Stories

I am grateful Scripture uses adoption as a metaphor for our new identity in Christ. In the ancient world, adoption powerfully conveyed the full acceptance and wonderful privilege of belonging to a new family. However, I have found that many people (myself included) struggle to fully attach to their new identity in Christ. They know the right answers but there's a gap between their knowledge and experience.

Sometimes people have a profound experience early on in their faith that helps them know exactly who they are in Christ. God's love has gripped them and they enjoy the steady love of God uninterrupted. For many people, however, coming to trust the truth is a progressive experience. And some may doubt and wrestle and question if they really are loved, cherished, and accepted by God in Christ.

I find it helpful to keep theologian and evangelist John Wesley in mind. He had been a faithful Christian for a long time before his "heart was strangely warmed" and he rested in the assurance of God's love for him. The "who am I?" question is not easily settled even if you know whose you are. So what can we do when we struggle to rest in our identity?

First, we anchor ourselves in the truth. Profound truth can quickly become familiar. Perhaps you've heard that you've been made in the image of God more times than you can count—and so hearing it yet again doesn't do much for you. You know you've been redeemed and adopted. But as we anchor ourselves in the truth, we can ask God to grant us wonder and awe. I hope I will never be someone who scoffs at seeing a sunrise or sunset yet again. May this be true for us regarding the beautiful truth contained in Scripture as well.

Second, we engage in the identity question with others. Since God made us for community, we discover who we are in relationship with others. One of the most vulnerable questions you can ask another person is, "How do you see me?" We can be oblivious to how our misguided stories are disrupting our identity in Christ. But trusted people can point it out. We can also be blind to the beautiful things God is doing in us. Once again, trusted people can draw it out of us. In some instances, the misguided story that is robbing you of joy and peace in Christ may need to be untangled through spiritual direction or professional counseling.

Third, we pray for God to affirm his love for us again and again. God pours his love into our hearts so that we can cry out "Abba! Father!" (Rom 5:5; 8:15). Let's ask God to keep his promise and word.

My wife, Julia, has followed Jesus since she was eleven. But a few years ago she realized she had never really asked God if he loved her specifically. Every day she started to pray, "Do you love me, Jesus?" It wasn't a demand or an accusation. She didn't set a time limit for Jesus to answer. She just wanted to hear from him about herself. She prayed, she pursued, she persisted.

About a month into this prayer, the Gospels came up in her daily readings, specifically the sections about the Passion of Christ. As she read these familiar passages that led up to Christ's death, she thought to herself, *I know this. I don't want to read it again.* But she pressed into the passages. Then she felt a very strong impression—words that were not her own: "I died so that I could be with you forever."

These ten words now hang at the entryway of our house. Julia cherishes them in her heart. She can still lose sight of this truth in her day-to-day life. She might not always be aware of how true it is. But this experience and truth is one she returns to again and again.

While I can't tell you how God will affirm his love for you, I can tell you that God's love for you is unchanging and available. Pray until he answers. Sometimes God reveals his love in dramatic ways. But from my experience he tends to go with subtleties. Why does God tend to whisper instead of declaring his love *Say Anything*–style with a boom box? As I once heard the pastor Craig Groeschel say in a sermon, "God whispers because of how close he is to us." If you want the dramatics, look to the death and resurrection of Jesus. There you will see God's love profoundly on display. If you want to hear it for yourself, wait for the whisper.

May you know your belovedness in Christ in a meaningful and life-transforming way.

Discover Your Identity

Almighty Father, in you we live and move and have our being. You are the author of life, the perfecter of our faith, and the Father of every tribe and nation: thank you for adopting us into your family as beloved sons and daughters. Please fill us with your Holy Spirit, that we might join the church throughout the ages and the world today in crying, "Abba! Father!" May we be quieted by your love and have ears to hear your loud rejoicing over us. We pray that you would root and ground us in your love. Help us to rest in who you declare we are, through Jesus Christ our Lord. Amen.

Take a moment to pray

Sit quietly with God for five to ten minutes. Ask the Spirit to guide your reflections. Write down a brief prayer in your own words for this section:

Misguided Stories

There are many kinds of misguided stories, such as self-authorship, performance, or contamination stories. Take time to identify and describe a few of the misguided stories that have shaped your identity. Start by asking: Who wrote this story for you? Who does it say you are? How does it affect you?

I summarize two of my own misguided stories as "almost but not enough" and "exciting but wrong." How would you summarize yours?

_____

_____

_____

_____

_____

_____

_____

Redemptive Identity

Below are a few ways Scripture further describes who we are in Christ. Circle words that resonate the most with you.

Accepted	EPH 1:6	Innocent	EPH 1:4
Adopted	ROM 8:15	Justified	ROM 5:1
Beloved	JER 31:3	Kept	1 PET 2:25
Blessed	EPH 1:3	Loved	JN 15:9
Child of God	1 JN 3:1	Masterpiece	EPH 2:10
Chosen	EPH 1:4	Never alone	DEUT 31:8
Coheir	ROM 8:17	New creation	2 COR 5:17
Conqueror	ROM 8:37	Not condemned	ROM 8:1
Delighted in	ZEPH 3:17	Righteous	2 COR 5:21
Delivered	COL 1:13	Sanctified	1 COR 6:11
Forgiven	EPH 1:7	Set apart	1 PET 2:9
Free	GAL 5:1	Washed clean	IS 1:18
Friend	JN 15:15	Whole	COL 2:10
Healed	1 PET 2:24	Wonderfully made	PS 139:14

How do these truths about who you are in Christ dismantle your misguided stories?

_____

_____

_____

_____

_____

_____

_____

_____

Engage your imagination: When God sees you, who does he see?

_____

_____

_____

_____

_____

_____

_____

_____

_____

_____

_____

_____

_____

_____

_____

_____

Choose one meaningful word or image that connects you to your redemptive identity:

_____

Reflect: What did you take away from this section?

Jot down any key insights or aha moments, or topics for further study and learning:

_____

_____

_____

_____

2

Gifts, Talents, and Personality

Now to each one the manifestation of the Spirit is given for the common good.

1 CORINTHIANS 12:7

Spiritual gifts are the presence of the Spirit Himself coming to relatively clear, even dramatic, expression in the way we do ministry. Gifts are God going public among his people.

SAM STORMS

I WAS SEVEN WHEN MY GRANDFATHER DIED. When his will was read, my family was surprised that he had left his carpentry tools to me. But it made sense to my young mind. I spent hours with my grandfather playing in the backyard. We pretended to embark on daring missions. He built me a fort. He fashioned me swords and shields (much to my mom's displeasure). He fostered my imagination. Then he was gone and I possessed two large chests of tools. For many years, they collected dust in our workshop. Sometimes I would open them to rummage for a tool. But everything in them was mostly unused.

Decades later my parents moved and we had to decide what to do with these chests. I felt the freedom to take a few items as keepsakes and to give the rest away. I trusted that my grandfather didn't care if I became a carpenter. If I had misunderstood his intention I might have felt pressure to become one, or perhaps even guilty for not living up to his desire. But the gift of the tools of his trade was a message for me. I am certain my grandfather wanted me to remember how the tools opened up a world full of joy and love.

In other words, the tools mattered. But not as much as how they made space for our relationship to flourish.

Through my grandfather I learned that carpentry requires a specific set of tools, each designed for a particular task. Seasoned carpenters wouldn't use the length of their hammer to measure something instead of a measuring tape, nor would they use a utility knife instead of a chalk line to mark cuts. From the plane to the saw, chisels to the squares—they all work together. When each tool is used for its unique purpose, the hands of the carpenter can craft something beautiful, like a sword and shield for an imaginative boy with dragons in his sights.

It's similar with God's gifts.

God gives all of his children distinct gifts, talents, and personalities. Every person has a unique part to play within the family of God. But sometimes our gifts go unidentified or unused. They collect dust like my grandfather's chests of tools. Or we pick up a tool and can't identify it. Is it a spiritual gift or talent? Sometimes we're not sure how to use what is in our hands. As we open or reopen the treasure chest of God's generous gifts and explore what's available to us, I want you to remember that the gifts matter, but not as much as what they create.

The intention of the Gift Giver matters more than the gift itself.

Every gift from God is good and an expression of his love. They are given to build us up in love so that the church grows in maturity and increasing Christlikeness (see Eph 4:1-16). And when we all work together, uniquely expressing the treasure of our gifts and talents, God brings more beauty into the world.

Spiritual Gifts

The New Testament contains several lists of and references to spiritual gifts. Together they create an eclectic vision of how God equips us. The gifts include administration, apostleship, discernment, encouragement, evangelism, exhortation, faith, giving, healing, hospitality, intercession, knowledge, leadership, mercy, miracles, mission work, pastoring, prophecy, serving/helping, teaching, tongues, tongues interpretation, and wisdom (see Rom 12; 1 Cor 12; Eph 3:6-8; 4; 1 Pet 4:9-10).

The lists in the New Testament are not exhaustive, but they are the best place to start in discerning what kinds of gifts God gives to his church. And don't worry if you don't know what some of these gifts are; there are many resources available.[1]

Our theology for spiritual gifts comes primarily from a letter the apostle Paul sent to Christians living in Corinth (specifically 1 Cor 12–14). One reason Paul wrote to them was because they had begun to misuse spiritual gifts. Some specific gifts were being celebrated above others. They elevated some people and diminished others. But it was to their detriment. It was the equivalent of using a screwdriver to hammer a nail. Their gatherings looked more like pageants, and the parade of specific gifts overlooked the significance of all gifts.

The Corinthians had lost sight of the intention of the Gift Giver.

Paul's letter corrects their misuse. In a sense, it gives us his reactionary theology of gifts rather than his proactive thoughts. The letter reminds us that we can take good things and distort them, even spiritual gifts.

The idea that a spiritual gift could be misused might be surprising. But imagine a father who gifts a fly-fishing rod to his preteen daughter.

Due to inexperience, the daughter might use the rod recklessly and accidentally hook herself or her father. Because of her immaturity, she could use the rod as a weapon to hit someone. It will take time with the gift giver to learn to use the rod well and safely. In a similar way, because of our own inexperience, immaturity, and sin, we can misuse gifts. This was happening in the church in Corinth, and it still happens today. Yet our Father works patiently with us as we learn to use his gifts for their intended purpose.

Before I say more about spiritual gifts, it's crucial to recognize that the greatest gift God has given us is grace. The apostle Paul wrote to the church in Ephesus, "by grace you have been saved, through faith— and this is not from yourselves, it is the gift of God" (Eph 2:8). This immeasurably generous gift is coupled with the gift of the Holy Spirit. Jesus said, "If you then, though you are evil, know how to give good gifts to your children, how much more will your Father in heaven give the Holy Spirit to those who ask him!" (Lk 11:13). God is eager to give us grace and delights in sharing himself with us when we ask.

We also need to recognize that our worth has no relation to the spiritual gifts we receive. Please don't confuse your spiritual gifts with your value, or another's spiritual gifts with their value. You are valuable because God loves you. God saved you by grace and dwells in you through his Holy Spirit. Whatever gifts the Spirit gives to us have nothing to do with our worth and importance in God's sight. Rather, we are stewards entrusted to use the gifts wisely and well.

With these cautions in mind, I want to consider what Paul wrote about spiritual gifts to the Corinthians. He begins by reminding the church that there are many gifts but that they all come from the same source: the Holy Spirit. The Spirit gives and empowers spiritual gifts. Paul reasons that since every gift has the same source, they are designed to unify and not divide. The Spirit distributes gifts for our common good so that together we grow in Christlikeness (see 1 Cor 12:4-11).

Every single follower of Jesus receives gifts. Nobody gets left out. The Spirit decides which gifts are given to each person. Even so, it's right and good to earnestly desire gifts. We are even invited to ask God for specific gifts (1 Cor 14:1). God may honor that desire and give us the gifts we ask for. Or God may choose to gift us in other ways. But if God does not give us the gift we desire, it doesn't mean he hasn't given us gifts at all.

Pastor and author John Piper earnestly desires the gift of tongues. But no matter how many times he has asked to receive the gift, as he says, "The Lord always says 'No. I have given you a gift: a gift of teaching, preaching, and of shepherding.'"[2] Piper helpfully reminds us that although the Spirit "apportions as he wills," we have permission to continue to ask for gifts and to see if God will choose to give them to us (1 Cor 12:11).

I experience some gifts seasonally and others regularly. One of my seasonal gifts is words of knowledge. The Spirit gives me insight about someone that I could have not known naturally. I get an image or picture along with a word of exhortation or encouragement for them. In the early days of planting St. Peter's Fireside, I experienced this gift regularly. But as we became rooted and established as a church, and as God added more people, I experienced this gift less frequently. I wrestled with this and asked God what changed. Did I do something wrong?

I sensed that the answer was that God had brought more people to the body who could express the same gift. God didn't take the gift away. That isn't his style. He was simply making space for others to express their gifts.

Whatever gifts we may receive, whether we experience them seasonally or regularly, we are to see ourselves as individual parts of a whole. As Paul says, "You are the body of Christ, and each one of you is a part of it" (1 Cor 12:27). This picture of a human body helps us grasp how spiritual gifts are meant to function within the church. Paul continues:

Now if the foot should say, "Because I am not a hand, I do not belong to the body," it would not for that reason stop being part of the body. And if the ear should say, "Because I am not an eye, I do not belong to the body," it would not for that reason stop being part of the body. If the whole body were an eye, where would the sense of hearing be? If the whole body were an ear, where would the sense of smell be? But in fact God has placed the parts in the body, every one of them, just as he wanted them to be. If they were all one part, where would the body be? As it is, there are many parts, but one body. (1 Cor 12:15-20)

Each of us has a distinct part to play for the church's growth in Christ. Some gifts may be more visible while others operate behind the scenes. But every gift is indispensable. And any spiritual gift should be pursued in love and put to use for love. Because without love they are bankrupt and empty (see 1 Cor 12:31–14:1).

No person needs all the gifts because we need the entire body. Our interdependence frees us from coveting and from feeling insufficient. We don't need what someone else has because we are part of the same body. What they have isn't hoarded but offered for our mutual benefit. Nor do we need to try to be someone we're not. Our unique roles and gifts are enough. As long as our church has a healthy mix of gifts, together we will have all we need.

Discovering Spiritual Gifts

Since spiritual gifts play a vital role in our formation in Christlikeness, it is important to carve out time to identify and learn about our gifts so that we can best serve the church according to what God has given us.

If discerning your spiritual gifts is new ground, start with tracking any spiritual experiences and see if there is a pattern. As part of that process, try to identify three things: opportunity, response, and affirmation. Has God orchestrated opportunities for you? Have you responded to these opportunities in a way that highlights a spiritual gift at work? Have those you've served or people who have served with you affirmed this gift at work in you? Let's look at a few examples.

Erik lives in downtown Vancouver and is able to walk to work. Each morning he passes people who are homeless and without adequate shelter. In the past he had adopted the standard practice of averting his gaze and staying his course. But since he started following Christ, Erik has noticed a change in his heart.

Now when Erik encounters people on the street, he can't ignore them because they're made in God's image. Each person presents an opportunity for Erik to see and highlight their dignity, and a newfound compassion wells up in his heart. Slowly, he has learned how to respond to these opportunities. Sometimes he simply offers temporary company or a smile. He tries to learn people's names and then greets them each morning. Other times he buys them a meal, and if he has time he even sits down with them to eat. Sometimes he offers to pray with the people he's developed a rapport with. Erik has also built connections with shelters and other resources that he shares with people. And although it is rare, he eagerly helps people take steps to get off the street or find their way into overnight shelters. His prayer life has also started to change. He spends more time praying for the marginalized and the nonprofit sector that takes care of them.

The change in Erik hasn't gone unnoticed. Sometimes the people he helps on the street express gratitude for his sincerity and willingness to be interrupted. Some of the organizations have pointed out that Erik's compassion is unique and inspirational. And as Erik shares some of his stories with friends, they affirm him. They see how he has aligned himself with the kingdom of God and that God is working through him.

As Erik reflected on these opportunities, how he learned to respond, and the affirmation he has received, he discerned that he has the gift of mercy. And though every Christian shares the responsibility to care for the poor and marginalized, Erik has begun to discern how he can uniquely use his gift of mercy to do so.

Alyssa also carved out time to reflect on and discern her gifts. As she did so, she identified how often people confided in her and were comfortable doing so. Friends, acquaintances, and even coworkers would approach her to talk about a struggle or sense of hopelessness. Alyssa also took note of an unusual patience in her ability to listen. And she acknowledged that she knows what to share and how to help people connect with God. Even if people who came to her didn't share her faith, she could discern how to respond in a way that made faith plausible and attractive. And quite often, people tell Alyssa that her presence and what she shared was what they needed to hear, and that they even feel closer to God or interested in learning more about her faith.

As Alyssa reflected on these opportunities, how she learned to respond, and the affirmation she has received, she discerned that she has the gift of words of wisdom and pastoring.

Our experiences with spiritual gifts may be more subtle or overt. Regardless, when cooperating with God happens more seamlessly or effortlessly, we should take note. Similarly, if the unique ways that we follow Jesus influence our environment, it's likely we've exercised a spiritual gift.

But I want to caution you about putting too much stock in your feelings in a given moment.

If you feel good or bad, encouraged or discouraged, or if what you're doing feels easy or hard, exciting or boring, it is not always a clear indication of how God is or isn't at work. Since our feelings fluctuate, they are not always a reliable guide. We are called to follow Jesus through the highs and lows, in times of excitement and drudgery, and even when we don't feel much at all. Jesus and his commitment to us remain the same, even if our feelings tell us otherwise. Much of the time, we faithfully exercise our spiritual gifts in the pursuit of Christ and feel "normal."

With this caveat in mind, the primary positive emotions associated with the Spirit are peace, joy, and love (Rom 14:17). When you express a spiritual gift, these emotions will flow forth from time to time. However, the Spirit also feels deep pain, desire for us, and even healthy jealousy and unutterable groans (see Rom 8:26; Eph 4:25-32; Jas 4:5). These feelings of the Spirit are how God relates to the disorder and brokenness of our lives and the world. If we feel any of these things while exercising our spiritual gifts, it doesn't mean something is wrong; it may mean we're getting a sense of God's heart.

You can reflect on your spiritual experiences to identify spiritual gifts. But you can also serve and observe. Put on an exploratory mindset and seek different opportunities to serve. As you try things, ask God to show you when his gifts are at work. Invite people to tell you if they see your gifts at work too. Pay attention to when you feel close to the Holy Spirit. When we live into the ways God has designed us, we have a peaceful and joyful spiritual satisfaction.

Many of us will be at different stages in our knowledge of and experience with spiritual gifts; this is normal. It may take time to discover your spiritual gifts as you ask God to reveal them. If you see someone who appears further along in the process, ask them for guidance and help. And even if this is familiar ground for you, there is always space to grow and learn more about how God has gifted us.

Before we move on to our talents, I want to address three tensions that arise within a community exercising spiritual gifts. First, it's really tempting to treat certain gifts as more spiritual or advanced. Which gifts these are changes from circle to circle. In Charismatic or Pentecostal contexts, for example, speaking in tongues, healing, and prophecy can sometimes be more highly prized, whereas in Baptist or Presbyterian environments, the gift of preaching or teaching is elevated. It's not inherently wrong to value these gifts, but it is always wrong for the gift to become a status symbol or a mark of spiritual maturity.

Second, as we seek growth in spiritual gifts, we should listen to these words of wisdom from pastor Jon Thompson: "The gifts are normative but the experiences of them are not."[3] This means that someone with the same spiritual gift as you may experience it differently or express it differently. For example, one person with the gift of prophecy may receive prophetic words, while someone else may receive prophetic visions. Or people with the gift of teaching may have different methods and contexts. One may teach on Sundays, another at conferences, and yet another in a weekly community group. Don't write off a spiritual experience just because it looks different from someone else's.

Last, it's common to experience "gift tension" in community. Due to our unique spiritual gifts, we can focus our concerns and efforts on vastly different things. Someone with the gift of mercy might emphasize the need for the community to reach out to the poor and then may get frustrated when that doesn't happen. Someone with the gift of hospitality may put a lot of effort into church events, and feel perplexed or frustrated when others do not. We are each geared toward different aspects of ministry. When we keep this in mind, we can avoid conflict and ultimately work together to strengthen the church the way God designed.

Talents

Our talents are distinct from our spiritual gifts. Our gifts are a manifestation of the Holy Spirit's empowering presence in our lives. This sets them apart from our talents. Our talents are our natural strengths and developed skills that often overlap with our areas of interest. Some of our talents may come from inherent abilities or our given context, such as being athletically inclined, or being good at organizing groups of people because we come from a large family. Other talents are developed through training, schooling, practice, or discipline.

Although talents differ from spiritual gifts, they don't exist in isolation chambers. Instead, God often gives us opportunities to use our spiritual gifts and talents in tandem. Many gifts and talents can work together. For example, if you have the spiritual gift of hospitality and a talent for baking, the two could come together in a gloriously welcoming and delicious way. Or you may have the gift of teaching and be a talented writer, and so you write books and articles. Someone else with the gift of teaching may be a compelling speaker and so they find themselves invited to speak at public events. Often our talents and skills are vessels for expressing our gifts.

Sometimes our spiritual gifts so closely align with our talents that it's hard to tell them apart. You could have the spiritual gift of administration and also be a really great administrator because of your work experience and education. Or you may have the gift of wisdom and also be very well-read with loads of life experience. It can be difficult to know where the talent ends and the gift begins. It's likely a spiritual gift if you're using it in the context of the church; if there's opportunity, response, and affirmation; and if people are growing in Christlikeness as a result (either by your direct influence or your supporting role). But if you can't quite tell where your talent ends and your gift begins, don't worry about it too much. Focus on good stewardship. Whether it's a talent or a gift, everything is a gift from God to be used for his good purposes as we love and serve one another.

Even apart from our spiritual gifts, our talents can be used to serve the body of Christ and open doors for making him known in the world around us. Consider Bezalel and Oholiab. They were filled with the Spirit of God to make artistic designs for the tabernacle (see Ex 31). It's unlikely their skills and talent appeared out of nowhere. The Spirit filled them to use their talents for God's work. Similarly, a skillful graphic designer could use their talent for their church's social media accounts or promotional materials, which in turn could help draw people to the church. Someone financially savvy could help their church with budgeting and improve the way that they communicate about money. Although talents are not manifestations of the Spirit in the way that spiritual gifts are, God invites us to use our talents to serve him and others. They are part and parcel of the unique role we each have in the body of Christ.

Personality

Our gifts and talents shape how we participate in the body of Christ. But the body of Christ is not an amorphous, impersonal blob. Our personalities matter too.[4] Your uniqueness influences how you express your gifts and talents in community.

Your personality is the combination of characteristics and qualities that makes you distinct. Our biology, upbringing, environment, and experiences all contribute to who God made us to be. In the Psalms, David declares that we are "fearfully and wonderfully made" (Ps 139:14). God handcrafts each of us.

But David's poetic declaration is not the full picture of our personalities as expressed throughout the Bible. The apostle Paul speaks at length about the tension between our sinful nature and the Spirit (Rom 7–8; Gal 5). Yes, we are fearfully and wonderfully made, but sin has invaded our bodies and made our hearts desperately broken and unpredictably disordered (see Is 5:20; Jer 17:9; and Mt 15:19).

Our personalities are in the process of being redeemed. Until God brings his good work to completion (Phil 1:6), we are never fully ourselves. Whoever we are in this moment is at best a work in progress. But even in our imperfection, God loves us as his children. God doesn't love the future version of ourselves. He loves us as we are. The Spirit is at work day by day to renew our true selves—the people God made us to be (2 Cor 4:16).

For better or worse, our personalities influence what we do. For instance, they affect the way we experience God and express ourselves. We see this in different forms of prayer. Introverts may be more drawn to private, less expressive prayer, while extroverts may enjoy prayer that is more public and "charismatic."[5] Our personalities also inform what skills we are drawn to learn and what roles we wish to play. Some parts of our personality will complement our gifts and talents when we exercise them, while other aspects can inhibit them.

There are a couple of pitfalls we want to avoid when it comes to our personalities. One is the temptation to compare ourselves to others or allow ourselves to feel as if someone else is more spiritual or more connected to God because of their personality and the way they express their gifts or talents. There are forms of worship and service for the way God has made each of us, and all of them can be valuable to the body of Christ.

Another pitfall is pigeonholing ourselves into always doing things a certain way, or only doing particular tasks that fit who we are. While we should be mindful of who we are when it comes to expressing ourselves through our gifts and talents, God might surprise us with what he wants to do through us.

Sometimes God also challenges and stretches us. For example, God selected Moses to speak as his public prophet even though he had a speech impediment. And yet Moses' disposition toward anger had serious consequences for his ministry (see Ex 3-4; 32). God called the entirety of Moses—physical limitations, character flaws, and all. He works through our weaknesses and even redeems our failures.

We can't ignore the role of our personality in our call to follow Jesus. From a young age, I have been creative and audacious. These parts of my personality have allowed me to take risks and try new things. I have toured throughout Canada, moved across the continent, been part of a start-up design agency, and planted a church. But I am also stubborn. While my stubbornness has frequently been redeemed into perseverance, it has occasionally blindsided me.

When I went on my first tour at age twenty, my mom said to me, "I think this will be hard for you. You value your family too much." I thought, *You don't know me! You don't know what you're talking about.* But only a month later and halfway across Canada, I found a phone booth and made a collect call with a lump in my throat. At the sound of my mom's voice on the line, I started to cry. I stubbornly wanted the touring life. But I didn't see how it was misaligned with my deeper desire to be rooted in a place.

God has since rooted me in Vancouver as a pastor. Over the years I have discerned that my essential spiritual gifts are teaching and pastoring. I am also a talented graphic designer and communicator. And leadership is one of those areas where I have a tough time discerning between gift and talent—it's taken a lot of hard work to develop. I have seen the Spirit bring my gifts, talents, and personality together to serve the church and world.

But I also have a depressive streak. I can ruminate on hurt, fail to see the good, and drift toward nihilism. Even my brokenness has been redemptive though. My experience with depression has motivated me to advocate for mental health within my church.[6] My openness about my mental health challenges has made space for others to be courageous in sharing their struggles. My pain has also deepened my empathy as a pastor. God has made me a wounded healer.

I see a thread God has woven in me. I am still the imaginative boy whose heart is set on fighting battles for the sake of good. And I will use all the tools available to me in God's treasure box to seek the beauty of his kingdom on earth as it is in heaven.

May you see the unique ways God has made and equipped you with gifts and talents for the sake of building others up in love.

Discover Your Gifts, Talents, and Personality

God our heavenly Father, every good and perfect gift comes down from you, in whom there is no shadow: thank you for the gift of knowing you and your grace. Please fill us with your Holy Spirit and grant us eyes to see and receive the gifts you've entrusted to us. May we steward every gift and talent according to the ways of your kingdom. You have uniquely made us. Please give us vision for how we can each use our gifts and talents in many different ways for the common good of the church and for the sake of the world. Help us not to hold onto your generous gifts, but to hold fast to you, through Jesus Christ our Lord. Amen.

Take a moment to pray

Sit quietly with God for five to ten minutes. Ask the Spirit to guide your reflections. Write down a brief prayer in your own words for this section:

Reflect on these spiritual gifts

Slowly consider this list and research any unfamiliar gifts.

Administration	Knowledge
Apostleship	Leadership
Discernment	Mercy
Encouragement	Miracles
Evangelism	Mission Work
Exhortation	Pastoring/Shepherding
Faith	Prophecy
Giving	Serving/Helping
Healing	Teaching, Tongues
Hospitality	Tongues Interpretation
Intercession	Wisdom

In the recent past, how have you experienced God working through you for the benefit of others? If you don't know, take time to pray and reflect on what God may want to show you:

. . . Now discern your spiritual gifts

Revisit the spiritual gifts list. Cross out gifts you do not have and circle ones you do have.

Known gifts

_____

_____

_____

Possible gifts

_____

_____

_____

Desired gifts (even if crossed out)

_____

_____

_____

Reflect on your gifts

Be still with God for a moment. Select three spiritual gifts that are significant to you. For each one, consider the following questions:

1. Can you recall a time when you put this gift into action?

2. When you use this gift, does it move people toward Jesus?

3. Has anyone affirmed this gift in you?

_____

_____

_____

Write down your talents and skills

Circle the talents you could use to serve the church. Start with ones you easily get absorbed in doing.

Make it practical

Prayerfully consider how you can use your spiritual gifts and talents to serve the church and benefit others.

_____

_____

_____

_____

_____

_____

_____

What words consistently describe you?

Circle words that describe you at your best, and draw a square around words that describe you when you're not your best.

Achiever	Bold	Dependable	Gluttonous
Active	Calm	Despairing	Gregarious
Adventurous	Competent	Disorganized	Happy
Affable	Competitive	Emotional	Humble
Affectionate	Conscientious	Energetic	Imaginative
Aloof	Controlling	Entitled	Indulgent
Altruistic	Courageous	Exuberant	Intellectual
Ambitious	Covetous	Fair	Irritable
Angry	Creative	Fearful	Jealous
Anxious	Critical	Fearless	Joyful
Audacious	Curious	Fun	Keen
Bitter	Cynical	Generous	Kind

Lustful	Passive	Shy	Talkative
Meticulous	Persistent	Smart	Tolerant
Moody	Practical	Sociable	Trusting
Nervous	Punctual	Spontaneous	Valiant
Open	Quiet	Strong-willed	Warm
Organized	Reserved	Supportive	Worrisome
Original	Rigid	Suspicious	
Outgoing	Sensitive	Systematic	

In your average, free, best, or Spirit-filled moments, what are you like?

_____

_____

_____

_____

_____

_____

In your low, stressed, worst, or sinful moments, what are you like?

_____

_____

_____

_____

_____

_____

_____

Write a brief summary of your whole personality:

Make it practical
How might your personality positively affect how you express your spiritual gifts and talents?

How might your personality negatively affect how you express your spiritual gifts and talents?

Reflect: What did you take away from this section?

Jot down any key insights or aha moments, or topics for further study or learning:

3

Virtuous Values

*Seek his kingdom and his righteousness, and all
these things will be given to you as well.*

MATTHEW 6:33

*During the first ten years of my life, the only
clear thought I had was "get candy."*

JERRY SEINFELD

MIDWAY THROUGH 2015, the leadership team of my church added
a new line item to our budget: pastoral development. It was generous but also a gracious nudge toward growth in some of my weaknesses. We had gone through a difficult staff transition. It became
clear I could benefit from some leadership and personal development. I had no complaints.

I took a nine-month certificate course in values-based leadership.
It was mostly online, but it included two weeklong stays at Hatley
Castle on Vancouver Island. Once again, I had no complaints. This
is the same castle that appeared as the X-Mansion for four of the
X-Men movies. It made for a stunning learning environment. Between sessions I walked along paths through immaculately curated
gardens. I was calmed by the view of the Pacific Ocean. It was the
perfect space to digest what I was learning.

During the course, I learned a lot about values. I named my per-sonal values. I collaborated with my church to identify our values. I developed values for our staff. I drank deeply from the waters of values.

But I also became aware of how a lot of books and articles about values embrace a world of our own making. Some even turn values into a quasi-spirituality that can fix everything.[1] The hype around values sells the story, "If people, leaders, organizations, and governments can get their values straight, the world will manifest its full potential."

Not quite.

But values do matter.

When I first named my values, it was like receiving a map (or cell reception) after driving around aimlessly for far too long. I may have ended up at my location eventually or by chance. But with a map, I knew how to get there.

We navigate life with our values. But rather than fill our plate with preferred values from a buffet of our own creation, Jesus invites us into values that align with the kingdom of God. As we align our values with what God desires, we develop virtuous values.[2]

What Are Values?

Everyone has values. But what exactly are they? Here are a few ways different people define values:

- "Values are a shorthand method of describing what is im-portant to us at any given moment in time."[3]

- "Values are deeply held views of what we find worthwhile."[4]

- "Values are ideals that give significance to our lives, that are reflected through the priorities we choose, and that we act on consistently and repeatedly."[5]

Values describe what is important and worthwhile to us. They don't just influence how we think, but also the quality of how we live. But each definition also shows the subjectivity of values. They are what any person happens to value, at any time, for any reason.

So what do values look like in practice?

In one of his sketches comedian Jerry Seinfeld jests, "During the first ten years of my life, the only clear thought I had was 'get candy.' That was it. Family, friends, school—they're just obstacles in the way of the candy."[6]

I still haven't outgrown this value.

Seinfeld is exaggerating, of course. But he helps us get a sense of how values operate. They are like a compass leading us to our true north, even if that place is a swimming pool filled with Sour Patch Kids.

But eventually we "put away childish things" (see 1 Cor 13:11) and discover values that pull us upward toward higher pursuits.

David was the ruddy shepherd boy with beautiful eyes who grew up to be a poet, warrior, and king. Although imperfect and broken, he was "a man after [God's] own heart" (1 Sam 13:14). Throughout his life he was deeply committed to the presence and ways of God. He valued faithfulness.

Before David inherited the kingdom of Israel, he was driven into exile. He spent his time on the run from the mentally afflicted and soul-tortured King Saul, hiding out in caves and even living among Israel's enemies. But he refused opportunities to harm Saul—not just once but twice. David was faithful to the ways of God and didn't dare lift his hand against his anointed (1 Sam 24:6; 26:9).

At the height of his success, David's deepest yearning and desire was to build a house for God. But when God said no and told David that it would be his own son who would build the temple, David remained faithful to his desire to honor the Lord. He put aside the resources Solomon would need (2 Sam 7; 1 Kings 7).

Even at his low points, David returned to his value of faithfulness as his true north. He abused his power and coerced Bathsheba into bed, and then he covered up her pregnancy by having Uriah murdered. But when the prophet Nathan shook him back to his senses with a parable, the first words David uttered were, "I have sinned against the LORD" (2 Sam 12:13). Then he prayed, "I was sinful at birth, sinful from the time my mother conceived me. Yet you desired faithfulness even in the womb" (see Ps 5). Once again, there it is: faithfulness.

Faithfulness helped David navigate his life—the complex moments, the mountaintops and successes, and even horrific failures. Faithfulness acted as his map and compass, directing him toward God's presence and ways.

Aspirational and Actual Values

David knew faithfulness was important to him. But our values aren't always obvious to us. If you ask a child what they value they will likely shrug, even with a mouthful of candy. Or you might wonder why you get upset when your spouse forgets to commemorate the anniversary of the first time you shared five-and-a-half minutes of uninterrupted eye contact. It could be because you value celebration, and you expect your spouse to share your values—even if you haven't named them.

When we start to name our values it becomes obvious that some of them are aspirational. We desire to attain them. Other values are actual. We embody and live by them.

Let's say you're the loyalist who is unmovably faithful to people—even to a fault. You put dogs to shame. You're the kind of person who is going to stand in someone's corner whether they're winning or losing the fight. You will be there for a friend through mistakes, even if they let you down. You won't give up. Inversely, your value of loyalty can also explain why it hurts so deeply when people make decisions that do not appear to support you in the best way, or when people fail to show up when it matters most to you. If this is the case, it's fair to say that loyalty is an actual value for you, as it explains your actions and expectations.

However, if you say you value loyalty but you're not all that reliable, you talk about people behind their backs and you're always looking out for *numero uno*—well, it's an aspirational value for you. The desire is good. But the desire needs to give birth to action. You will need to acknowledge your shortcomings and grow before you make loyalty an actual value. Values are only actualized when they're supported by consistent effort and habits.

It's not all or nothing; some of our values are aspirational and others are actual. But we need more than values of our own creation. It's not enough to merely pick and choose what we prefer. Our values need to be anchored in something beyond ourselves. Otherwise how do we know if they are good or worthwhile? How do we know if we're aimed toward higher pursuits? Theologian and pastor Sam Storms writes, "Gazing at the grandeur of heavenly glory transforms our value system."[7] This is where virtuous values come in.

Virtuous Values

The most famous teaching of Jesus is the Sermon on the Mount (Mt 5–7). Many values are highlighted throughout the Sermon, such as mercy, peacemaking, and humility. For example, Jesus teaches, "Be careful not to practice your righteousness in front of others to be seen by them. If you do, you will have no reward from your Father in heaven" (Mt 6:1). As he applies this to common disciplines like giving, prayer, and fasting, he calls us to value integrity and faithfulness.

Since our values are what are important and worthwhile to us, it's fair to hear Jesus calling us to bring our values into alignment with his kingdom and calibrate our sights toward him. He does that explicitly in the Sermon on the Mount. In fact, if I were to summarize the Sermon with one sound bite from within it, it would be: "Seek first his kingdom and his righteousness, and all these things will be given to you as well" (Mt 6:33).

But Jesus doesn't only want us to desire his kingdom. He also wants us to embody his ways. He wants us to develop actual kingdom values.

In several of his letters, the apostle Paul reflected on the values of God's kingdom and how they take root in our lives. The Spirit develops fruit in us: love, joy, peace, patience, kindness, goodness, faithfulness, gentleness, and self-control (Gal 5:22-23). God even creates desires within us that were not previously there and gives us the will to fulfill them (Phil 2:13). But we aren't merely passive recipients of kingdom qualities and values. Elsewhere, Paul encourages us to actively "put on" these same qualities too (Col 3:12-17). We put in some effort. But aspirational values of the kingdom only become actual values by God's initiative and help.

Throughout history, Christians have not typically tried to create their own values. That's because they have been in pursuit of virtue. The Catholic Church has a helpful definition of virtue in their catechism: "Human virtues are firm attitudes, stable dispositions, habitual perfections of intellect and will that govern our actions, order our passions, and guide our conduct according to reason and faith. They make possible ease, self-mastery, and joy in leading a morally good life."[8] At first glance, this sounds a lot like some of the definitions for values. But the major difference is that virtues have nothing to do with subjectivity.

Virtues are transcendent. They cut through the confusion of a world where everyone determines reality for themselves. We don't get to choose for ourselves what is good or bad and right or wrong. Virtues are not a matter of choice. There is a universal standard set by God.

The virtuous person is firm, stable, and consistent because they are anchored in a life outside of themselves. They habitually do what is good, not in their own estimation but in the sight of God. When our actual values align with the kingdom of God and his righteousness, they are virtuous values.

Toward Virtuous Values

As part of my doctoral research I had the pleasure of interviewing Harper on her life story.[9] I loved the two hours I spent with her. We sat by the large window in her comfortable apartment on a rainy but bright Vancouver day. As we sipped coffee, I asked questions and listened.

Among other topics, Harper told me about the moment when she decided enough was enough. Several years prior, she had taken an honest look at her life and concluded that she wasn't a good role model for her daughter. She wanted to be. But for the better part of a decade, she had stopped growing as a person and wasn't taking care of herself. It was hard for her to admit, but being a good role model was only an aspirational value.

As Harper retold parts of her life story to me, she identified how losing a job in her early twenties was a defining moment. Although she had been a leader for much of her life, she internalized a message that she wasn't a leader. Over time she accumulated some counterproductive values like security and self-protection as ways of avoiding risk and hurt. She learned to play it safe and keep her head down. These became her actual values. And they were undermining her.

Harper didn't change overnight. It was more like a five-year journey. She brought her actual values to light, named her aspirational values, and began walking with Jesus down a path of healing, learning, and growth. The woman I sat with had embraced risk, gone back to school, stepped into leadership, become an entrepreneur, and fostered holistic well-being along the way. She had intentionally explored her values as part of her transformation and started to lay aside actual values that weren't in alignment with the kingdom of God. Over time her aspirational values became actual values.

She can now say that being a role model for her daughter is an actual value.

The Challenge of Values

Sometimes, like Harper, we see an actual value and it's not pretty. It's holding us back. Because some of our values are misaligned with who God has made us to be and the ways of the kingdom. Some values require recalibration through repentance and others require death through crucifixion.

Our values can also clash. The reality is that two competing sets of values are at work within us. The apostle Paul describes an ongoing, daily conflict between the old self and the new self, our sin nature and the Spirit (see Rom 6–8). Writing to the church in Ephesus, he said: "Put off your old self, which is being corrupted by its deceitful desires, and . . . be made new in the attitude of your minds, and . . . put on the new self, created to be like God in true righteousness and holiness" (Eph 4:22-24).

The values of the "old self" are patterned after the ways of our wider culture and world. These values can be corrupted through deceitful desires. They are misaligned with God's kingdom. Whereas the values of the "new self" reflect the likeness of God and the life he shares with us through the Spirit.

Even seemingly positive values can be misaligned. Author and values expert Richard Barrett acknowledges that even good values can have a "shadow side." For example, the value of loyalty can make a person prone to in-group thinking or reluctant to admit someone is deeply wrong. The value of security can make someone stingy with their resources. The value of financial stability could lead to hard work in an attempt to provide for others or give generously, but the same value may lead you to take advantage of others or steal to get by. Sometimes leaders champion values like unity, gentleness, and meekness, but in reality, they are attempting to silence conflict rather than engage it with openness and integrity.

Sin can manipulate our values for selfish purposes, causing us to embrace values contrary to the kingdom and to our own detriment. The quality of any value depends on its calibration—Who or what is it aligned to? Is it self-serving or modeled after the ways of Jesus? Is it patterned after the wider culture around us or seeking after the kingdom? Is it dependent solely on us or empowered by the Spirit?

When we are driven by values that do not orient us toward the kingdom of God, it's likely that they are part of our "old self." As a result, we will participate in "works of the flesh." Paul describes these works, or actions of our sin nature, as "sexual immorality, impurity and debauchery; idolatry and witchcraft; hatred, discord, jealousy, fits of rage, selfish ambition, dissensions, factions and envy; drunkenness, orgies, and the like" (Gal 5:19-21). These activities flow out of our hearts (Mt 15:10-20). They are the product of sin. But rarely do we stop to think about how our values might factor into the equation. Sin can cause our values to become misaligned. It can express itself in values such as indulgence, self-interest, and recognition—which can lead to the "works of the flesh."

None of us escape the tension of sin's influence upon our values.

When my church went through our difficult staffing transition, the first churchwide meeting we held to talk about what happened went very poorly. I earned a failing grade. It was a hard meeting, and it only created confusion and bred distrust. We were less than two years old as a church plant and suddenly our idealism walked out the door.

When I went into that meeting, I hoped to create space for people to be heard and ask questions. I wanted to assure people that nothing nefarious had taken place. I intended to acknowledge hurt and disappointment. Our leadership team wanted to provide as many answers as we could. I thought the end result would build trust. But when the opposite happened I was left confused.

What went so wrong?

After learning about values, I saw how the "shadow side" of values got the best of me. Thanks, hindsight. I genuinely value open and transparent communication and listening well. But I went into that meeting using these values to solve the issue and put it to rest. I wasn't prepared to communicate what needed to be said. And I wasn't really interested in listening well. What happened?

Well, more fundamentally, sin worked itself out through my values. I was defensive and self-protective, because I was concerned about my reputation and ambition to grow a church.

Thankfully, a seasoned businessman and member of our church pulled me aside and offered to connect me with a consultant who could help. I was grateful to work with Gregory. He taught me to name what went wrong and chart out a path to try again. Our church was surprised and gracious when I admitted publicly how I got it wrong and asked for an opportunity to try again. Our second churchwide meeting was an entirely different experience.

As my experience of the first meeting reveals, the "shadow sides" of values and sin are sneaky. We don't always see what is happening when they're taking place. This means that identifying whether our values are orienting us toward the kingdom of God or not requires the voice of Scripture, prayerful discernment, and ongoing repentance, all in the context of spiritual friendship in the church. But this does not need to be burdensome. Because Jesus delights in teaching us his ways, walking with us on the journey, and giving us countless second chances.

Constellation of Values

There are many values. One values expert says there are 125 that can be identified in most cultures. The average person selects about twenty-five of them. And on any given day we prioritize somewhere between five and eight values, often unconsciously.[10] If we want to bring more intentionality to our values, it's recommended that we simplify by keeping only three to five values at the forefront of our attention.

It can help to think of our values like a constellation. Imagine stargazing on a clear night. We can never take in the whole sky. We can't number the stars. But we can learn to find and name some constellations like Orion, the Big Dipper, or Draco. Each of these constellations is made up of its own stars. And all of them are part of the totality of space. Constellations help patterns of space come into focus in a unique way.

This is how values work too.

We can't embrace every value. We can only look through a telescope at the vastness of values and zoom in on a few at a time. But it does help to name our current constellation of values, and how it is aligned or misaligned with the kingdom. We don't need to permanently limit ourselves to only a few; there will be seasons when we turn the telescope and focus in on a new constellation. But it is important to know what values are at the forefront of our attention at the moment.

When I went through the values-based leadership training, I identified five core values: truth, community, well-being, making a difference, and humor. For each of these values I wrote a statement:

- Telling stories that are true
- Crafting community that's real
- Living in and out of well-being
- Giving people a story to tell
- Laughing until our sides hurt

These values and statements came out of self-reflection. But even after naming these values, some fit and others didn't feel quite right. A few pointed me toward the kingdom, whereas others felt more like projects in self-fulfillment. (I was also enamored with "story" at the time.)

A few years later, when my church first started running rhythms for life retreats, I identified my five values as truth, interdependence (community), well-being, making a difference, and family. As you can see, most of my values remained the same, but there were small shifts—continuity but also change. Because that's how growth works. When I reworked my values statements, though, I tried to make their connection to the kingdom more explicit (at least to me):

- ◆ Truth is our compass.

- ◆ We are better together.

- ◆ Lead out of health.

- ◆ Develop people.

- ◆ Be intentional with family life.

When it comes to the ways of Jesus, we cannot fully comprehend the breadth of kingdom values. They are vast like the stars and sky. We shouldn't presume to name every kingdom value any more than we should think we can align ourselves with all of them.

But our limitations shouldn't mean that we dismiss familiarizing ourselves with kingdom values as much as possible. There is always, always, always more to learn about the kingdom of God. We can ask God to help us name our current constellation. And we can look through our telescope at the kingdom and try to make sense of how we see it today.

Naming Your Values

You don't need to sit down and come up with a list of values that will last until your eighty-seventh birthday. Give yourself permission to explore. Try asking yourself what values reflect who you currently are and who God is inviting you to become. What values uniquely express who God has made you to be and how he has gifted you? These are the questions that "values stargazing" in the kingdom requires.

As you name your values, seek to discern how they are aligned or misaligned with the kingdom. As you do, you will see how God is shaping you and pulling you toward himself. Because God is already creating the desire for virtuous values in you—and he can give you the will to live them out too.

May you desire the kingdom and embrace the values that draw you into the virtues of Jesus.

Discover Virtuous Values

Almighty Father, you are the great King above all kings: thank you for sending your Son, Jesus Christ, into the world to make your kingdom known among us. We join the church throughout the ages in praying, "Your kingdom come!" As we await the return of the King, increase our desire for your kingdom. May we seek first the kingdom as we walk in the ways of Jesus. By the power of your Spirit, help us to value what draws us ever closer to you and to repent of all that draws us away, through Jesus Christ our Lord. Amen.

Take a moment to pray

Sit quietly with God for five to ten minutes. Ask the Spirit to guide your reflections. Write down a brief prayer in your own words for this section:

Discover your values

Select nine values that are very important to you. Focus on values you consistently act on. If there are words that better describe your values, use them. Circle values you actively seek to embody in your life. Be ruthlessly honest with yourself as you complete this activity.

Achievement	Family	Optimism
Adventure	Financial Stability	Partnership
Advocacy	Friendship	Passion
Ambition	Generosity	Patience
Authenticity	Goodness	Peace
Balance	Grace	Play
Beauty	Growth	Pleasure
Caution	Helping	Power
Celebration	Honesty	Productivity
Challenge	Hope	Respect
Collaboration	Humility	Risk
Community	Humor	Sacrifice
Compassion	Independence	Safety
Competence	Influence	Security
Competition	Innovation	Self-Control
Contemplation	Integrity	Skillfulness
Continual Learning	Interdependence	Strength
Control	Joy	Teamwork
Courage	Justice	Tradition
Creativity	Kindness	Transparency
Development	Leadership	Trust
Diversity	Loyalty	Truth
Efficiency	Making a Difference	Vision
Empowerment	Mentorship	Vulnerability
Ethics	Mercy	Well-Being
Excellence	Moderation	Wisdom
Faith	Openness	Worship

Rank your values

Write your top nine values in alphabetical order in column [1-9] and write them in the same order in row [A-I]. Compare the first value [1] with the first value [A]. They are the same so the square is shaded. Now compare value [1] with value [B] and decide if value [1] is more important to you than [B]. Put a + if it is more important than [B] or a - if it is less important. Do this for the remaining values, and then proceed to [2] and repeat the process. Once you have a + or - in all the boxes, add up the total number of +s for each value and then rank them from highest to lowest.

Values	A	B	C	D	E	F	G	H	I	TOTAL
1										
2										
3										
4										
5										
6										
7										
8										
9										

Bring your top five values together

RANK	Values
1	
2	
3	
4	
5	

Try values statements

State each of your top five values as a single sentence. For example, if you have humor listed as a value, you might write "Laughing until our sides hurt." (Tip: Try stating them positively without using negations.)

Reflect on how your values are misaligned with the kingdom

What is the shadow side of your values? How might they be misaligned with the kingdom of God at times? For example, if you have security as a top value, how might it cause you to shrink back from the risks God asks us to take in trusting him?

Reflect on how your values are aligned with the kingdom

How might your values connect you with the kingdom of heaven? For example, if you have making a difference listed as a value, how might this value connect with the Great Commission?

_____

_____

_____

_____

_____

_____

_____

_____

How might aligning your values with the kingdom of God free you from sinful patterns and shortcomings in your life?

_____

_____

_____

_____

_____

_____

_____

_____

Dream a little

Just like people, values are dynamic, not static. It's important to aspire toward desired values. And it can help to have a single focus. Is there anything God is stirring in you? Is there one value you would like to prayerfully pursue more intentionally in your life and embody?

What is one value you wish to see more of in your life?

_____

Reflect: What did you take away from this section?

Jot down any key insights or aha moments, or topics for further study or learning:

_____

_____

_____

_____

_____

_____

4

Roles

*Here's what I want you to do, God helping you: Take your
everyday, ordinary life—your sleeping, eating, going-to-work, and
walking-around life—and place it before God as an offering.*

ROMANS 12:1 *THE MESSAGE*

God does not need your good works, but your neighbor does.

MARTIN LUTHER

I CAN'T RECALL WHEN I DECIDED that I wanted to be a musician.
But once I did, there was no turning back. I wasn't a particularly
gifted musician. But that didn't stop me. I was driven by the elation
of performance.

Throughout high school I played in some unimpressive bands.
Over a four-year stint after graduation, my band recorded some
songs, released two EPs, and toured, mostly around Western Canada.
If the measure is generous, I was by some measure a "professional"
musician. When I awoke covered in flea bites from sleeping on the
floor somewhere in the middle of Canada, I knew I was well on my
way. When we started building a relationship with a record label, I
felt like I was really a musician. The role was officially mine.

But after almost five years of hard work, my band parted ways with me and signed with the label. Although I knew they made the right call, it was still painful and deeply disorienting. It felt like the role was taken away from me. I lost a sense of myself. And since most of my friendships revolved around music, I felt isolated. After that I toured one more time with another band across Canada. And then it was over. I put down the role of being a musician. On some level, though, I had always known it was a role that never really fit.

With my tail between my legs, I went back to school and studied graphic design. I took on the role of a student. And once I graduated, I took on the role of a designer. In this new role, I was quite talented—a welcome change. With some unhealthy pride I enjoyed saying I was an "award-winning" designer. I played the role of "arrogant elitist" with ease. I worked at some interesting advertising agencies and exciting design firms. I received some accolades and praise. Eventually though I put down this role as well in order to welcome a new role: pastor and church planter.

To be clear, I've never had just one role at a time. None of us do. All along the way I've had many different roles: son, sibling, friend, boyfriend, prankster, and occasional nuisance. I've added the roles of husband and father to that list, and have several other current roles as well. One way to think about how many roles you have is by the names you have. I am "Daddy" (father), "Love" (husband), "Canon Sterne" (only Anglicans will understand), "Al" (exclusive to blood family and childhood friends despite my chagrin), "Boykie" (by my South African parents), and "Alastair" (friends).

All of our roles in life matter, but they are not all equal in importance. Some have undue importance at times. Some get taken away or put down. But each and every role shapes us. I no longer actively play the role of musician or graphic designer, but I've retained the skills from those roles and stories.

Sometimes I look at the accumulation of my past and current roles, though, and wonder, *How do all these fit together?* They look like an eclectic patchwork quilt of random colors, shapes, and patterns that I'm not sure should go together. I can see that they're all connected, but I'm not sure I understand the whole. How do my many roles relate to who I am?

The answer is that our identity is uniquely lived out through our roles. All of our different roles can come together as a harmonious whole when they express our uniqueness in Christ through our gifts, talents, personality, and values. In other words, it's through our roles that the rubber meets the road as we live into and out of our identity day after day.

What Are Roles?

Everyone has roles. Shakespeare wrote, "All the world's a stage, and all the men and women merely players. They have their exits and their entrances, and one man in his time plays many parts."[1] I want to clarify, though, that I am not referring to a role as pretending or acting or putting on a mask. A role is a unique way of being in the world and relating to a person or group.

For example, the role of a spouse is a unique way of relating to one person, and the role of a student is a way of relating to peers and a teacher. Every single role is unique because it carries its own set of expectations, behaviors, and values. Most of us slip in and out of many different roles unconsciously throughout our days and weeks. We have many wardrobe changes and are accustomed to wearing many different hats. However, all of our roles together shape the contours of our lives. They factor into what makes each of us unique.

Let's look at this through an amalgamation I'll call Tom. He doesn't need an alarm because like clockwork his four-year-old daughter wakes him up at six every single morning without fail. She bounces on Tom with incredible enthusiasm and eagerness to begin her day with milk and Cheerios, *stat!* Tom jumps out of bed as daddy before he's even brushed his teeth.

Although he may be a little sleep-deprived and bleary-eyed, Tom enjoys his breakfast routine with his daughter. While they eat, his wife is also getting ready for work. She has an important meeting today and shares some of her anxieties as she moves about the house collecting her things, mumbling to herself, "Phone. Purse. Keys. Phone. Purse. Keys." Tom switches into his husband role. He offers his wife some encouraging words, points to her keys, gives her a kiss on the cheek as she leaves, and nudges his daughter to give Mommy a hug and kiss goodbye. Half an hour later, Tom drops off his daughter at preschool. In his role as parent, he mingles with other parents and chats with the teacher before jumping on the bus with thirty other commuters—which makes him highly aware of his role as a city dweller.

As Tom walks into the office, he steps into a whole host of roles related to his career. The receptionist sees Tom as his boss, the CEO sees Tom as her employee, and Tom's email inbox reminds him of his sometimes daunting role as a human resources director. At noon, Tom meets an old friend for lunch and steps into the friend role. Around three in the afternoon, Tom's phone pings with a text from his dad in Korea who wants to catch up. He is reminded of his role as a son, and on some level, his role in Canada as an immigrant. Then at five, Tom heads home and reenters his roles as daddy and husband, albeit a more tired version of them.

This snapshot names just a few of Tom's roles, but I hope it helps you to see the many ways we engage the world around us. Tom has the roles of daddy, husband, parent, city dweller, boss, employee, HR director, son, immigrant, and friend. And he lives out these roles in a variety of places: home, the office, his daughter's school, the bus, and a restaurant. In each role, Tom engages people in a different way and often in a different place.

If you briefly reflect on your own life, you can probably identify many roles you play. Like Tom, you probably move in and out of them seamlessly throughout the day. But how do all these roles come together? How do they create a coherent picture of who you are?

Identity and Roles

Our roles can move beyond different hats we wear throughout the day or week or year. Each and every role is an opportunity to know God and uniquely express our identity in Christ. When we know how our roles reveal part of God's character, we can discover a new set of expectations, behaviors, and values. And as we do this, the way we relate to others in our roles begins to reflect the kingdom of God.

The idea of roles is present throughout Scripture, starting in the book of Genesis. In fact, God himself has many roles.

God is three persons in one nature: the Father, the Son, and the Holy Spirit. The three persons of the Trinity are equal in nature. But each of them has unique roles.[2] For example, the Father sent the Son into the world. These roles cannot be reversed. The Son does not send the Father into the world. Similarly, the Father sits on the throne and the Son sits at his right hand. Jesus has the role of Messiah, Son of Man, and Suffering Servant. He was crucified and resurrected—not the Father or the Spirit. The Spirit has the role of being sent by the Father and the Son as our paraclete or comforter. He also has the unique ongoing role of convicting the world of sin and transforming people in Christlikeness. If roles are important within the Trinity, they are important in our lives too.

Throughout Scripture, God's character is further revealed through human roles as metaphors: for example, God is a nursing mother, a divine warrior, a bridegroom, and a lover (see Is 49:15; 64; Mt 25:1-12; and Song of Songs). The Psalms overflow with images of God as various workers that affirm his care for creation and his ongoing creativity in the world: God is a composer, metalworker, garment weaver, gardener, shepherd, builder, chef, and wine-maker.[3] God has created roles in such a way that each one can tell us something about his character. Each role is also an avenue to reflect something about God's truth, beauty, and goodness into the world around us. God created roles for this purpose.

Our various roles are creative spaces where God affirms our identity in Christ with particular color and shape. In his endless creativity and love, God wants you to know him through each of your roles and to use each role as a channel to shower his love upon the world. Every role can become a piece of the mosaic that reveals Christ in you and through you for the sake of others.

Let's return to our friend Tom.

Imagine that Tom has read this book and is beginning to grasp his identity in Christ more deeply. When Tom prayerfully discerned his "meaningful word" in the identity worksheets, he landed on *accepted*. God's full and non-negotiable acceptance of Tom as his adopted son, by grace and not by works, resonates deeply with him and brings him into a fresh experience of the gospel. He no longer has to worry about saving face, nor does he have to worry about bearing shame, because God has bestowed the full honor of sonship on him. Tom now feels more freedom to acknowledge his short-comings and sins and to rest confidently in God's grace like never before. But how might Tom's identity as accepted in Christ be expressed in his daily life through his roles? What might change?

For starters, Tom begins to think more deeply about his role as father and his unconditional love for his daughter. Even if he is tired and at his wits' end, in the depths of his being he knows he is committed to what is best for her. He is more often eager to embrace her and hold her than reprimand her. As Tom considers this, he sees a glimpse of how his heavenly Father looks on him with an even greater love and commitment to Tom's own flour-ishing and good. And he knows that he has the great privilege of modeling the Father's love to his daughter. Tom's identity as ac-cepted by God also challenges him not to favor his daughter for her obedience (which he can be inclined to do) but for simply being his child. He wants her to grow up with the knowledge that his own acceptance of her is a small but vital glimpse of God's willingness to embrace her.

Tom also sees how his role as son needs some restoration. He notices how God's acceptance of him by grace is a truer story than his parents' acceptance, which was contingent on his success in school as a child. Even as an adult, they more often want to talk about what Tom is accomplishing in his life than how he is. But as Tom grows in his trust of God's acceptance, he finds that he is less driven by the desire to impress his parents. And although he cares about what they think and feel, he isn't as easily rocked by their disapproval or high expectations. In fact, a new desire has emerged in Tom's heart: he wants his parents to discover a more gracious way of relating to him and to each other. It'll take time, and he's not sure how it'll happen, so he starts praying for it.

At work, Tom sees how God is calling him to honor his receptionist and repent of subtly using shame to motivate those who report to him. And as a husband, Tom begins to feel permission to release the pressure he puts on his wife to pretend everything is okay between them when they both know it's not. His acceptance in Christ begins to take the burden off of his marriage to ground his identity because he now knows who he is first in God's eyes. Tom therefore feels free to acknowledge his failures, repent, seek healing with his wife, and even ask for help from a counselor.

Each of Tom's roles offers a unique space for him to grasp the gospel in a particular way and for God to present Tom as his accepted child to the world. His story helps us see how God works powerfully through roles to release his grace into the world. Our roles, in turn, further illuminate our identity in Christ and grant us the joy of walking in the good works of the kingdom God has marked out for each one of us (Eph 2:10).

The Proper Role of Roles

Roles are good gifts from God. They matter and are important in our self-understanding and our relationship with God. And as Tom's story shows, we have the opportunity to offer our roles to God for redemptive work in the world.

Yet we can allow our roles to stray from this intended purpose. If any role becomes the foundation for our identity, for example, we will struggle to rest in the freedom of being adopted into God's family. If we overemphasize them in any unhealthy way, our roles can overshadow and distort who we are in Christ. When this happens they are no longer subservient to Christ but play master over us instead.

Roles make bad masters.

"Sin isn't only doing bad things, it is more fundamentally making good things into ultimate things," writes pastor Tim Keller. He continues, "Sin is building your life and meaning on anything, even a very good thing, more than on God. Whatever we build our life on will drive us and enslave us. Sin is primarily idolatry."[4] Keller helps us see that it is sinful to make good things like our roles—as parent, employee, friend, or musician—into ultimate things. Because then the role is usurping the role of God, which is idolatry. And over time, if we build our lives on a role, it will drive us and enslave us.

Take the role of wife.

This is a significant role designed by God that provides meaning and challenge, joy and sorrow, and growth in Christlikeness in a woman's life. This role can help her grasp who God is and how God has uniquely made her. It is meant to be a vehicle of God's grace for a woman to know the love of Christ. And as a wife, she has the opportunity to model the church's love for Christ in the way she loves her husband (as well as demonstrating Christ's love for him) as a gift to the world around her.

However, if this role becomes foundational to her sense of self, it will overshadow her identity as an adopted daughter of God. If it

becomes her primary source of meaning and worth—if it is the ultimate thing she lives for—it takes the place only God deserves and
becomes an idol. The end result is tragic. The role of wife is corrupted from a good gift into a source of bondage. What was meant
to be an avenue for God's grace instead becomes a bar to achieve, and
an endless battle with comparison.

When good things become ultimate things, they fail over time
because we are not using them in alignment with their intended
purpose. It's like using a butter knife as a screwdriver—it will work
to twist in a few screws, but not over time. Imagine building an
entire house this way. Likewise, when a role becomes an ultimate
thing, it may work to give us a sense of meaning and purpose for a
while, but over time it will fail.

When a role is an ultimate thing, we must succeed at it—however
we define that—to ensure our worth. This relentless burden is what
enslaves us. If we fall short of "success," we're left in shame: *I'm not
good enough. I can't even treat my kids well.* If we meet and surpass our
goal, we're at risk of pride: *I'm clearly the best parent here. Just look at how
well-behaved my kids are.* Either position is weak and temporary. The
next day, the drive to prove ourselves begins again.

The only basis for your identity that will not enslave you in this
never-ending cycle of performance and comparison is the identity
you receive from God. You are adopted by him. You cannot earn it.
God has lavished his love fully on his children and spoken eternal
belonging and peace over those who are called to his grace.

Roles also cannot function as our ultimate thing because they
are temporary. They change and shift over a lifetime. When we
move out of a role that has functionally operated as our god, we will
be shaken to the core. I went into a tailspin when my role as a musician ended. My entire life was structured around music. Re-
hearsals, shows, recording, and endless promotion. Once it was
gone, I was disoriented. I lost a sense of purpose and meaning and

began struggling with suicidal ideation.[5] The grief related to the loss was appropriate. It is normal to experience loss, and grief even, when important and significant roles change, such as when you change careers, retire, or lose your spouse. But the existential despair I experienced signified that the role had a disproportionate importance to me.

God's vision for our lives as Christians is that we have purpose and hope grounded in him that goes deeper than even our most important roles. When our roles shift or even end, we must grieve the loss while holding on to the hope that the role (as important as it has been) is not everything. God will use other avenues of grace in our lives to continue working out his redemptive purposes in us and through us.

Simply put, roles are not meant to receive our deepest affections and worship. If we make a role our ultimate thing, it will crumble and fall, like the house of the fool who built his foundation on sand (Mt 7:24-27). Only when God names us and speaks words of identity, adoption, and grace can we find rest and peace in the care of Jesus Christ, the shepherd and overseer of our souls (1 Pet 2:25). When our roles are subservient to him, they can become a reflection of him.

Role Tension

We can experience tension in specific roles or unfulfilled roles, or we may feel strained when our many roles conflict.

Even if we seek to reflect Christ in each of our roles, we are not guaranteed flourishing in all our relationships. We can improve our part in a relationship and sometimes not see any change. How are we to handle this tension, whether it is the role of a spouse, parent, friend, or child? The apostle Paul wrote, "If it is possible, as far as it depends on you, live at peace with everyone" (Rom 12:18). We can only take ownership of our part. And we can continue to seek God's guidance and wisdom as we live into the tension. Many of our roles will always have tension because they involve other people.

But then there is the tension of unfulfilled roles. This can be especially hard when it comes to the roles of spouse and parent. Are there any roles you hope to have? It's important to name them. It's okay to grieve a role you've never had and long to have. And it's okay to hope. But when you're in the tension of unfulfilled roles, guard your heart against making them into an idol and invite trustworthy friends into the pain.

We live as people with many roles and limited time, energy, and capacity. We constantly face decisions about which roles to prioritize: Do I call my sister or my best friend tonight to catch up? Do I stay late at work to finish a project, or do I go to my daughter's ballet performance? Do I go to the studio to work on a painting after work, or do I surprise my girlfriend with coffee? The right decision isn't always clear. There is no set list of rules to follow. Navigating tension between roles often looks more like asking honest questions before God and your community, getting your priorities straight, and addressing the tension as it arises.

Julia graciously reminds me that I made vows before God to her before I made vows to God as a pastor (and the ordination liturgy in the Anglican tradition involves a lot of vows!). But even if these vows had happened in the reverse order, I believe God wants my role as a husband to have a greater priority in my life than my role as a pastor. It's the same when it comes to my role as a father to my two daughters. I once read that roughly 50 percent of retired clergy wish they had spent more time with their families. I've taken this to heart. But the tension between the roles of husband, father, and pastor is real and at times difficult to navigate. It does me and those I love no good to deny that this tension exists. Instead, I need to be in an ongoing conversation with my wife and trusted spiritual friends about the tension so we can discern what the best balance is for the season we are in.

When we set out to plant a church in Vancouver, BC, Julia and I had an ongoing conversation/debate about how many hours a week were appropriate for work related to the church plant. Julia thought it should be a more conventional number of hours, like any job, and I argued that it should be informed by the culture of a start-up. We found a modestly stable middle ground and it worked for a while. But the conversation was never really over.

When our first daughter was born, we almost immediately had to revisit how much time I spent working. Late one night, Julia said in frustration, "You have so much vision for our church and so little vision for our family." In that moment she touched on the deeper issue. It was painful to hear. And I didn't like to admit it, but she was right. We could have only made this discovery by addressing the role tension we were experiencing, not pretending it wasn't there. I could have said and meant, "I value my role as a husband and father *above* my role as a pastor." But the lived experience was different. In practice I valued my role as a pastor above all. The way I invested my time had to change, but more fundamentally my vision had to change. I needed greater vision for how our family could reflect the image of Christ together.

Tension between our different roles is unavoidable. Sometimes we strike a healthy balance and sometimes we are oblivious to how we say one thing yet live another way. Press into these tensions, because through them, God is revealing his ways to us. And no matter what, Jesus sustains the universe (Heb 1:3) and holds all things together (Col 1:17)—even our roles.

May you discover how your roles can reflect God to your people and place.

Discover Your Roles

God, Most High and Holy, three in one, Father, Son, and Holy Spirit: You have revealed yourself as three persons in one nature. You help us in our finitude to grow in our understanding of your infinite nature by revealing yourself in roles. May we come to see how each role we are entrusted in life can reveal more of your image in us. Please shine brightly through us and reflect your love through our roles for our people and place. Help us become glimpses of the world that is to come, through Jesus Christ our Lord. Amen.

Take a moment to pray

Sit quietly with God for five to ten minutes. Ask the Spirit to guide your reflections. Write down a brief prayer in your own words for this section:

List all the roles in your life

_____   _____

_____   _____

_____   _____

_____   _____

_____   _____

. . . Now whittle down your roles to five

If there are more than five roles that take up significant time and energy, consider if any can be eliminated or minimized for better life balance. Realistically, you cannot simply eliminate life-draining roles. Some of the most important non-negotiable roles in our lives can have life-draining aspects to them. Sit with the Lord and ask him for discernment.

Discover role tension

In the "actual prioritization" column below, list your roles in order of how much time and energy they actually absorb. In the other column, list them in order of how you think they should ideally be prioritized. Ask God to reveal any role tension and to guide you in finding a healthy balance, one that represents his love for you and all people.

Actual Prioritization   **Ideal Prioritization**

_____   _____

_____   _____

_____   _____

_____   _____

What changes might you need to make in your life to relieve some of this role tension?

_____

_____

_____

_____

_____

_____

_____

_____

_____

Do any of your roles have an unhealthy importance in your life? If so, how?

_____

_____

_____

_____

_____

_____

_____

_____

How can each role express your identity?

Each of your roles is subservient to your identity in Christ. No matter how life-giving or life-draining, each role is an opportunity for you to connect to the image of God in you and to express God's image to others. Brainstorm with God here. What can each role teach you about who God is, and how might you demonstrate that to others as you live into it? If you need ideas, think about how Tom connected his roles to his identity in Christ.

What current role gives you the clearest image of Christ? What current role gives you the blurriest?

Reflect: What did you take away from this section?

Jot down any key insights or aha moments, or topics for further study and leaning:

_____

_____

_____

_____

_____

_____

_____

_____

_____

_____

_____

_____

_____

_____

5

Vocation

I have come that they may have life, and have it to the full.

JOHN 10:10

*The word vocation is a rich one, having to address the
wholeness of life, the range of relationships and responsibilities.
Work, yes, but also families, and neighbors, and citizenship,
locally and globally—all of this and more is seen as vocation,
that to which I am called as a human being,
living my life before the face of God.*

STEVEN GARBER

"IT'S NOT ABOUT YOU."

This is the opening line of the world's biggest-selling book in 2003 and 2004, *The Purpose Driven Life* by Rick Warren. It sounds counterintuitive to the stratospheric individualism of the Western mind, but purpose is found beyond ourselves. The success of Warren's book is evidence that many of us long for purpose in life. If we know why we are here, it helps us stay focused and infuses life with meaning.

In his book *Start with Why,* author and consultant Simon Sinek writes, "Very few people or companies can clearly articulate why they do what they do. By why I mean your purpose, cause or belief—why does your company exist? Why do you get out of bed every morning? And why should anyone care?"[1]

So, what is your purpose, your why?

Traditionally our purpose has been called our vocation. Vocation comes from the Latin word *vocare* meaning "to call." Our purpose is a call from beyond ourselves: a calling from God.

When it comes to the Christian life, calling is often misunderstood as "the call" to ministry (narrowly understood as pastoral work) that those with supersonic Holy Spirit–hearing receive. Undoubtedly this specific call happens for some people. (If you want some help to discern such a call, flip to "A Simple Guide for Discerning A Call to Ministry," appendix C.) But this is only one of many ways God calls. Don't falsely assume that only some get "the call" or that any other expression of God's call is lesser than the calling to vocational ministry.

God has a calling for every single one of us. Vocation refers to the way God works in and through each of us, using the gifts he has given us, to bring flourishing to his creation, in all the roles and settings he has placed us in.

Simply put, our vocation is our identity uniquely lived out before God.

Vocation is a singular call from God. But the call is multilayered. Each layer acts like a tuning dial on an old transistor radio that helps reduce static. As each layer is dialed in, the fuzzy noise is reduced so we can hear the call. The different layers of vocation help attune us to our vocation.

Creational Vocation

The first layer of vocation is creational. When God created us in his image, he called out to us, "Be fruitful and increase in number; fill the earth and subdue it" (Gen 1:28). Our creational vocation is the call to pursue the flourishing of people and the world. This is the call of every single human who has ever walked upon the face of the earth.

From the relationships entrusted to us to the homes we have built, from the sidewalks we walk on to the schools we create, from the fields and animals that provide us food to the restaurants we visit, and from the law courts to upholding justice in society—God invites us to add our personal touch to all that he has made. We do this through our God-given mosaic of roles. Whether you're an artist, plumber, teacher, parent, architect, flight attendant, politician, waitress, lawyer, or anything else, your roles are opportunities to respond to your call.

Our creational vocation makes us, as Steven Garber writes, "responsible, for love's sake, for the way the world is and ought to be."[2] But we do not always contribute to the flourishing of the world. We also add to its dysfunction.

Since the image of God in us has been vandalized by sin, our creational vocation has been tarnished too. We pollute, confuse, and distort creation in the process of living as sinful people. We create amazing technologies like cars and smartphones but compromise the environment and our psychological well-being at the same time. All that we have done or left undone (as the Anglican confession goes) contributes to, or compromises, our ability to fulfill our creational vocation. Because we live in a fallen world, we need a redemptive vocation that can heal the image of God in us so that we move away from compromising the well-being of creation and toward contributing to its goodness and flourishing.

Redemptive Vocation

Our redemptive vocation is the call of Jesus: "Follow me." This is the second layer of vocation. Often when we think of faith, what comes to mind are the things we believe: the different tenets or doctrines of our faith such as the Trinity, the inspiration of Scripture, justification, and so on. Of course, faith involves what we believe, and what we believe is important. But the life of faith is initiated with a call, "Follow me." This call requires a response. We move in the direction of Jesus.

In the ancient world of Judaism, when a rabbi invited a disciple to follow them, the goal wasn't merely instruction but transformation. A disciple was expected to sit under their rabbi's teaching and know their take on a life with God. But they were also to become like their rabbi; think like your rabbi thinks, do what your rabbi does. When Jesus called his first disciples, this would have been the mutual understanding. If we follow Jesus and move in his direction, the expectation is that we will become like him.

But very quickly we discover that the path of discipleship is not possible by our strength alone. Can we love God with all our heart? Can we love not only our neighbors as ourselves but also our enemies? Can we accept ridicule and harassment as a blessing? Can we forgive as Christ has forgiven? Jesus shows us what it means to be human without the fractures and fissures of sin. How can we live up to him?

We do not walk into this call alone. We cannot. Jesus walks with us. He promised to be with us "to the very end of the age" (Mt 28:20). And he is always before us, behind us, and beside us. When he returned to the right hand of God, the Father and the Son sent the Spirit as our helper (Jn 16:7). The word for helper is *paraclete,* which refers to someone who comes alongside to strengthen. We only need to open our hands and ask for his empowering presence.

With each step we take toward Jesus, the Spirit empowers us to become like him. The call to follow Jesus is how our creational vocation is restored so we can contribute to the flourishing of all people and the world. Our transformation takes effort on our part but is empowered by the Spirit at work in us. Without our redemptive vocation, our creational vocation would perpetually be in disrepair.

Missional Vocation

As our redemptive vocation restores our creational vocation, our missional vocation emerges. This is the third layer of vocation. The mission of God is simply love on the move. Love dances among the Father, Son, and Holy Spirit. Because of his unstoppable love for us, even when we were at our worst, God sent his Son into the world to reconcile us to himself (Rom 5:6-8). Now that we are reconciled, we share in this eternal movement of love. Our missional vocation is joining God's love on the move as we make Jesus known in the world—to live as citizens of the kingdom of God, and as ambassadors who demonstrate what it looks like to walk with the God who is lovingly reconciling all things to himself (2 Cor 5:7-21). God's love does not stay still. The gospel always comes to us on its way to somebody else.[3] The good news about Jesus is an "explosion of joy."[4]

Your missional vocation changes how you live your daily life because *why* you live changes in light of Christ's call. The good works God has prepared for us to walk in are meant to shine before others (Phil 2:12-16). Everything we do in our ordinary lives can be infused with God's presence and love. In this we demonstrate not only how the world was meant to be but also what the world to come will be like. Inevitably, others will take note. This is why Jesus called us salt and light in the midst of a watching world (Mt 5:13-16).

And when others take notice of our lives, our lips are to always be "prepared to give an answer to everyone who asks you to give the reason for the hope that you have. But do this with gentleness and respect" (1 Pet 3:15). As we follow Jesus, our lives will require an explanation. Henri Nouwen said, "My deepest vocation is to be a witness to the glimpses of God I have been allowed to catch."[5] Jesus is alive and at work in our lives and the world. Our missional vocation is to embody this good news of great joy as we share our experiences of Christ with others and invite them into the movement of God's love in Christ.

Personal Vocation

We all share the same creational, redemptive, and missional vocation. But each person will have a unique expression of this calling. Your personal vocation is how your creational, redemptive, and missional vocation come together in *you*, and it's the fourth layer.

God knows you specifically and not generally. God knows you by name and knows the distinct ways your heart and mind more readily connect to your identity in Christ. God knows your talents and has given you spiritual gifts that respect how he has made you and also stretch you to continue growing into who you are becoming in Christ. God knows your aspirational and actual values and virtues, the struggles and strengths of your heart, and how you can uniquely contribute to the world as you seek first his kingdom.

The challenge of discernment. To discern your personal vocation is to discover the unique vision God has for you as you follow Jesus Christ. Sometimes you'll know in your bones what it is. Other times it feels mysterious and cloudy. Let's consider three reasons why discerning your personal vocation can be challenging.

First, we exist in a noisy world. "There are all different kinds of voices calling you to all different kinds of work" writes Frederick Buechner, "and the problem is to find out which is the voice of God rather than of Society, say, or the Superego, or Self-Interest."[6] It takes time and effort to silence the chatter around us in order to discern competing or misleading voices, as well as which motives are driven by self-interest or selfish ambition. If you struggle to hear God, remember that you need to create space and time to quiet all of the noise.

Second, we are always a work in progress. Since God's call on our lives is dynamic, it's not merely a matter of discovering something buried within us. The discovery of our personal vocation requires us to discern who God is calling us to be and what God is asking us to do in a given season. This necessitates self-reflection. But too much self-reflection can cause confusion. And introspection for its own sake is often like getting lost in the deep of the woods. Since we are in the process of becoming ourselves in Christ, we can't fully discover ourselves; the answers aren't there yet. If you get stuck in self-reflection, remember that no person can ever know who they are entirely. But it's okay; God always knows you better than you know yourself—and he has called you to himself.

Third, the work of discerning your personal vocation is not figuring out what you'll do for the rest of your life—but it's easy to get stuck here too. To be fair, God often directs us to our work. And sometimes vocation and career line up. But if we narrow our sense of calling and vocation down to only what we do and where we do it, we've set our sights too small. Because our vocation isn't always the same as our career. Our careers may radically shift as life progresses. Even the place God calls us to may change occasionally. Jesus simply calls us to follow him. He doesn't tell us where we will end up if we do. If you've struggled to discern your personal call because of needless pressure to "get it right" or find the "perfect" career, take a breath. God is always capable of course-correcting us, even if we make a mess or miss where we should have gone.

Where to Begin

Where should you begin then?

Jesuit priest James Martin suggests that "the first step in this journey is recognizing that our deepest desires are [often] holy desires planted within us by God."[7] Jesus has a unique purpose for your life that you discover on the path with him. Start by "listening to your life." Take note of the valleys and peaks. What stirs your sorrow and your joy? Buechner advises, "The place God calls you to is the place where your deep gladness and the world's deep hunger meet."[8] Pay attention to your gladness and empathy for others and you can begin to hear God's call.

My dapper British friend Bub entered into a season of rediscerning his vocation.[9] He spent a decade of his career as a structural engineer but felt a stirring for different work. Over many months, Bub created space and time to pray and discern. He went to networking events and informational interviews. He had countless conversations with his wife and friends. He read books, took courses, and tried new things. This all helped but didn't bring clarity.

When Bub paid closer attention to what stirred his heart, however, he moved toward his vocation. He noticed he felt deeply upset by unkept buildings or abandoned homes. As he listened to this part of himself, he realized it was a resurrection impulse—a longing to see God bring life out of signs of decay in our city. Bub began to look for work in development with an emphasis on projects that build community in a lonely city. After a year of searching, Bub didn't find his dream job. But he found his next right step as a project manager for a developer. He also began to volunteer in restoration projects around the city, which helps him stay in tune with his vocation.

In his helpful book *The Second Mountain,* David Brooks suggests another approach to discerning your vocation:

> The right question is not What am I good at? It's the harder questions: What am I motivated to do? What activity do I love so much that I'm going to keep getting better at it for many decades? What do I desire to do so much that it captures me at the depths of my being? In choosing a vocation, it's precisely wrong to say that talent should trump interest. Interest multiplies talent.[10]

What stirs our hearts? What keeps our interest? What gifts and talents do I bring to the table? All these questions can help us discern our personal vocation.

Sometimes, though, our vocation is birthed out of deeply painful moments where we finally encounter God's grace and forgiveness. This was true for the apostle Peter. Jesus called him and promised he would become a fisher of men (Lk 5:1-11). Jesus even promised that upon Peter he would build his church (Mt 16:18).[11] Talk about a vocation! But Peter didn't fully step into his vocation until he fell apart. Despite swearing it would never happen, and perhaps driven by self-preservation and fear, Peter denied knowing Jesus three times while standing by a charcoal fire (Jn 18:15-27).

After Jesus was raised from the dead though, he met Peter on the shores of the Sea of Galilee (conveniently at a charcoal fireside—see Jn 21). Over breakfast, their relationship was mended. Peter had denied knowing Jesus three times, so at the second fireside Jesus asked Peter three times, "Do you love me?" And three times, Jesus recommissioned Peter into his vocation with the words, "Feed my lambs. Tend my sheep. Feed my sheep." It was only after this second fireside experience that Peter stepped into his vocation. (This story is so meaningful to me that we named our church St. Peter's Fireside.)

Christ's love for us and our love for him propels us into our vocation.

Articulating Your Personal Vocation

The layers of our vocation can be expressed in thousands if not millions or even billions of enjoyable and different ways. Your personal vocation includes who Jesus has called *you* to be uniquely. I've found that articulating our vocation as we've discerned it can be a helpful exercise.

Malcolm Guite provides a helpful example for us. He is a poet, a singer-songwriter, an Anglican priest, and also an academic. He wears many different hats and has a few roles, but none are his vocation. In an interview he shared: "I went on a retreat in which I was asked to discern the heart of my vocation, as a person, not just a priest, and to write down in one sentence, the answer to the question 'why are you here?' I wrote 'I am here to use my love of language and my gifts with it, to kindle my own and other people's imagination for Christ.' That's still my mission and still the criterion whereby I make choices about what to do and what not to do."[12]

Unsurprisingly, Guite's personal "why" is beautifully articulated. His articulation of it helps him navigate how to follow Jesus. And his unique love of language and his gifts with it unite his different pursuits as a poet, singer-songwriter, priest, and academic. Clarity around his purpose helps him discern what to do and what not to do. But it's not only about him. He demonstrates a healthy balance of using his God-given wiring and gifts in a personally fulfilling way as he serves others for the sake of Jesus. His vocation is also for "other people's imagination for Christ." He is following Jesus on the path to abundant life.

It can help to see how others articulate their vocation. Here are a few statements people crafted during rhythm for life retreats at St. Peter's Fireside:

- "Breathe in oxygen, receive his grace, be present to his presence. Godspeed."

- "Hold space for others to share their stories and to reflect back to them the faithfulness of God in their lives."

- "Be a footnote in God's story and a wellspring of grace."

Whatever you write, keep it simple. You should be able to recall it easily without having to look at it.

Some people are more visual. Instead of writing a statement, a close friend of mine received a vision or picture of her purpose: "I saw a vision of me at the cross with Jesus allowing the Holy Spirit to guide my hand in pouring out the blood of Jesus. I understand this to be my vocation. The Holy Spirit guides me in bringing the healing of Jesus into the world." She's a mental health counselor, so it's obvious how this vision connects to her work. But it extends beyond her work. As a friend, I have firsthand experience of her vocation in the everyday ordinary moments.

Note, however, that as you try to put your vocation into words, the goal isn't just to write an affirmation statement of who you wish to be. This isn't about self-authorship or self-fulfillment. Rather, our vocation is received. We listen to God by paying attention to who he has made us to be and what he is calling us to do and where he is calling us to do it.

You might be wondering, *Isn't it enough to write "I am a child of God made for Christlikeness"?* It could be if those words enliven your soul. Whatever you write will be one of the infinite ways of expressing this fundamental truth. Don't be overwhelmed if you can't match Guite's clarity (he is gifted with language after all!).

And, again, while I think it's a helpful exercise, it's not necessary to reduce your vocation down to a statement or vision. It is somewhat artificial because our lives are more nuanced than one statement. The Reformer Martin Luther connected vocation to roles, and the purpose of every vocation is to love and serve our neighbors through our many roles—that's it. In this sense, he's right: we share the same creational, redemptive, and missional vocation. If you can't reduce your vocation down to a simple statement, start trying to write statements for a few roles and see if there are any common threads.

The Grit and Joy of Vocation

You'll find that identifying and intentionally stepping into your personal vocation involve grit and joy.

First, grit. As Brooks writes, "The summons to vocation is a holy thing. It feels mystical like a call from deep to deep. But then the messy way it happens in actual lives doesn't feel holy at all; just confusing and screwed up."[13] In the Western world, we're all too accustomed to ease. We begin to assume that if we've found "God's call" on our lives, the rest will be smooth sailing. But this isn't the truth. In fact, as Scott Cormode says:

> Over and over again when we Christians talk about calling we make a deal on behalf of God that God doesn't make. We say the deal is that you will get to do what you were created to do.

And we accidentally tell people, you will never have to do something you don't want to do. Every calling that is worth it encounters human beings . . . and sometimes human beings can be a pain and can be difficult.[14]

Our vocations always take place in a broken world amidst the joys and challenges of what it means to be human. And sometimes, living out our vocation is difficult. It requires resilience and endurance. You'll face challenges that you need to overcome and also challenges that will sometimes overcome you. There may even be times when you question whether you've been mistaken all along and somehow deluded yourself into thinking you found your call. But in the struggle, you'll learn, discover, and grow in Christlikeness. And your vocation will be refined.

The apostle Paul knew his personal vocation and still experienced hardship. He put it like this in his letter to the church in Philippi: "I want to know Christ—yes, to know the power of his resurrection and *participation in his sufferings*" (Phil 3:10 emphasis added). Even so, Paul could also write, "We are hard pressed on every side, but not crushed; perplexed, but not in despair; persecuted, but not abandoned; struck down, but not destroyed" (see 2 Cor 4:8-18). It's not all suffering. It's not all resurrection. It's both, working together.

Yet for all the grit involved in vocation, it also brings joy.

In my doctoral research, I interviewed urban Christians who were perceived by others as deeply joyful and who self-identified as joyful. I discovered that each participant had a deep sense of personal vocation. It turns out that living out of their vocation is connected to their joy.

This shouldn't be too surprising.

When we strip away the mystique of vocation, it is simply obedience to God. And Jesus promises us that when we abide (or dwell) with him—by which he means believe in him and obey his command to walk in his ways of love—the outcome is, as he said, that "my joy may be in you and that your joy may be complete" (Jn 15:11). Yes, there can be joy in contributing to the world and joy in finding a sense of purpose and meaning in what we do and offer to others. But the core reason our vocation results in joy is because it is simply another way to describe this experience of being with Jesus and doing what he says. As James Martin writes, "The closer one moves to God, the more one experiences a sense of deep joy."[15]

On one level, it would be nice if discerning our personal vocation were easier, wouldn't it?[16] And yet, in some sense, the mystery around discerning our call increases our relational intimacy and dependency on God. God doesn't want to give us a road map that charts out every step because he prefers to walk with us on the journey.

Personally, I've struggled to summarize my own personal vocation. I have a sense of what it is and I know when I'm walking in it. But words seem to escape me when I try to distill it down. Here's what I've learned: If you get stuck, stop trying so hard. Rest in the truth that Jesus has called you and is walking with you toward the end destination, which is Christlikeness. Jesus does not want to leave you in the dark. Even if you can't put words to your own personal vocation, Jesus will help you live it out as you walk with him in faith.

May you discover your personal vocation in Christ for the sake of others.

Discover Your Vocation

Almighty Father, you are the one who calls: You called Abraham to become the father of many nations. You called Moses to deliver your people. You called Isaiah and the prophets to be your mouthpiece for your wayward people. And you have called us all to yourself through Jesus Christ. As we follow him, help us to discover the vocation you have for us. Please grant us discernment and vision, that we might under-stand how we can uniquely express our identity before you. Amen.

Take a moment to pray

Sit quietly with God for five to ten minutes. Ask the Spirit to guide your reflections. Write down a brief prayer in your own words for this section:

Time to Review

Misguided Stories

Your Talents

Meaningful Word

Your Dream Value

Your Gifts

Your Values

Your Strengths   Your Weaknesses

Your Roles

Try to Summarize Yourself

In just a few sentences, summarize who God has uniquely made you to be at this moment in time. Here's mine as an example:

Although my misguided stories are "almost but not enough" and "exciting but wrong," more importantly I am known in Christ. I have the gifts of pastoring and teaching. My talents include graphic design, starting things, and leadership. I am creative and audacious. But I am also stubborn. I struggle with wanting to be the best and despair. I value truth, interdependence, well-being, making a difference, and family. I dream of being more joyful. I am a father, husband, pastor, author, and friend.

Your Deepest Desires

Listen to your deepest desires. Take time to name your joy and gladness as well as your sorrow and empathy for others.

What stirs your joy and gladness for others?

What stirs your sorrow and empathy for others?

Your Motivation

What are you motivated to do? What do you love so much that you're going to keep getting better at it for many decades?

Your Story

Like the apostle Peter, sometimes our vocation is birthed out of our most deeply painful moments where we encounter God's grace and forgiveness. Reflect on your own experiences of pain and grace and how they might be helpful for others:

Keep Asking Why

One way to find your personal vocation is to keep asking "Why?" Start with a significant role in your life, a deep desire, a motivation, or part of your story, and ask "Why?" For example:

Why do I want to be a lawyer? *To advocate for the weak.* Why is it important to advocate for the weak? *Because they are easily oppressed and this injustice angers me and God.* Why does this oppression anger you and God? *Because it isn't right.* Why isn't it right? *Because they deserve justice.* Why do they deserve justice?

Justice is for the weak; God intended for them to have justice. Why did God intend for the weak to receive justice? *Because God created people to be equal and to flourish.* So, what is your vocation? *My vocation is to join God's heart for justice in the world.*

_____

_____

_____

_____

_____

_____

_____

_____

_____

_____

_____

_____

_____

_____

_____

_____

_____

_____

Draft your vocation statement

What is your vocation? Why are you here? You might write a sentence, you might doodle, or you might just choose a few words that are meaningful to you. Shop around, try on a few outfits, and see if you can find language or images that work for you.

Now simplify it

What is your personal vocation? Why are you here?

Remember to keep it concise. It won't be helpful if you can't easily memorize it.

Part Two

Rhythms for Living Your Vocation

6

Crafting a
Rhythm for Life

Make every effort to add to your faith goodness;
and to goodness, knowledge; and to knowledge, self-control;
and to self-control, perseverance; and to perseverance, godliness;
and to godliness, mutual affection; and to mutual affection, love.
For if you possess these qualities in increasing measure, they
will keep you from being ineffective and unproductive
in your knowledge of our Lord Jesus Christ.

2 PETER 1:5-8

I must take care above all that I cultivate communion
with Christ, for though that can never be the basis of my
peace—mark that—yet it will be the channel of it.

CHARLES SPURGEON

WHEN YOU BUILD A HOUSE, YOU COULD WING IT. Head to the
hardware store, grab the materials you think you need—a box of
nails, some wood—and just go for it. But that probably wouldn't
turn out well for you. Even if you're skilled, there would likely be
code and safety violations. All in all, the entire enterprise would

be questionable. You need blueprints and a well-thought-out plan before moving into construction.

With the first half of this book behind you, you now have the blueprints to construct a rhythm for life. You'll want to keep referring to the blueprints to ensure you construct your life according to God's design. This isn't about self-authorship or shaping our lives as we see fit. Rather, we seek to identify and receive what God is already doing in us.

If you've struggled in the previous exercises, it's okay. It's normal to feel some tension, as if the answers you wrote down don't quite fit. You may find better words a week from now or a month from now. Or you might not. The point is not to perfectly articulate who we are and how God is moving in our lives. This isn't possible. We are not static people. We are in the dynamic process of being transformed. My hope is that the exercises have simply helped you start to find the weightier, more important things that sink to the bottom, like gold in a pan. But if things haven't settled yet, don't worry.

Wherever you are in the process, a rhythm for life is an intentional vision for pursuing Christlikeness. Does how we spend our life align us with God's purposes? The next step involves identifying spiritual practices for becoming who God made you to be.

Vision and Intentionality

Nobody arrives as a competitor at the Olympics by accident. And nobody will win bronze, silver, or gold without effort. It takes intentionality. The average Olympian trains for six hours a day, six days a week, twelve months a year, and consumes 1.1 million calories per year, which is equivalent to eating three Christmas dinners a day. A number of them have been working toward their goal for eleven years.[1] Beyond all of this, some even participate in intense psychological training, and practice visualization to improve their performance.

This sort of training is unfathomable for the average person. But that's because you're looking at the work rather than the prize.

Olympians have vision. They set their eyes on the prize. They know what they want and they commit to it. They structure their entire lives around it, intentionally giving up a lot of "normalcy." They can't live like everyone else.

The fact is that any vision worth your time requires intentionality, effort, and sacrifice. And your rhythm for life, specifically, requires vision and intentionality.

One of the most common struggles I hear as a pastor goes something like this: "I'm not reading Scripture, I'm struggling to pray consistently, and spiritual practices are hard for me." In my context of urban Vancouver, spiritual practices *are* often a struggle—I believe that. And yet many of the people who bring this struggle to me accomplish incredible things. They demonstrate discipline and intentionality in so many other areas of their life. It may be similar for you. If you've trained for a marathon, finished a degree, or found the job you want, or if you regularly feed yourself and keep up with your personal hygiene, you've done it because you have vision, intentionality, and discipline.

The issue for many people is not whether they can discipline themselves in an area. The issue is whether their vision is big enough to be worthy of sacrifice. If we lack discipline when it comes to spiritual practices, sometimes it's because our vision of God is too small.

The cultivation of our passion, love, or desire for God is, however, a two-way street, because we are not just "thinking beings" with brain-buckets for a dump of correct information. We are also desiring beings. James K. A. Smith writes, "The orientation of the heart happens from the bottom up, through the formation of our habits of desire. Learning to love (God) takes practice."[2] Although our vision fuels our intentionality and discipline, our intentional practices shape our vision and heart for God from the bottom up. What we do shapes how we feel and how we feel shapes what we do.

There's no escaping it: our faith requires effort. "Make every effort" wrote the apostle Peter (2 Pet 1:15). Even if you're faltering or weak in your desire for Christlikeness, intentional practices and effort can help reshape desires. And at the very least, they can create the space for you to bring your inner life honestly before God.

The Four Rhythms for Life

A rhythm for life is composed of four rhythms: up, in, with, and out.[3] Each reflects a different movement: upward to God, inward to self, withward in community, and outward in mission. Together they make up the rhythm for flourishing in the kingdom of God as we grow in Christlikeness.

For each of the four rhythms, I explore multiple expressions of three practices. The twelve practices are solitude with God, gratitude, sabbath, self-examination, stewardship, guidance, table, spiritual friendship, spiritual gifts, hospitality, generous service, and faith at work. My goal isn't to be exhaustive but rather to get you started with some essentials. If you want more ideas, see "Resources for Spiritual Practices" in appendix B.

While my examples focus primarily on spiritual practices, I don't want to give the impression that there is no overlap between "spiritual" and "general" practices. Some practices aid our well-being in general and others help us grow in Christlikeness. But both are integral to human flourishing. When approached in a healthy way, there is usually overlap. You may have a habit and discipline of exercising five times a week and a practice of praying throughout the day (perhaps even on your run!). Both are integral to your well-being.

It's also important to acknowledge that practices reflect the practitioner.

One way this occurs is when spiritual practices reflect our brokenness. Just as we can misuse the gifts God entrusts us, we can also misuse spiritual practices. We should not assume that because a practice *appears* spiritual it is forming us as it ought. For example, if someone struggles with an eating disorder, the practice of fasting could be deeply disordered. The practice of praying with others can become an outlet for gossip. As Jesus warns throughout the Sermon on the Mount, many practices (such as prayer, fasting, and giving) can be done for the wrong reasons, such as seeking approval from others or attempting to appear more spiritual than we are (see Mt 6–7).

Since every practitioner is a broken person in the process of redemption, it's best to look at our practices like *kintsugi,* the Japanese art of repairing broken objects. In kintsugi, instead of the brokenness of an object being hidden or concealed, the cracks are set with gold. In the same way, our brokenness and the way it can affect the practices we use does not need to be hidden but rather can be brought into the light. When this happens, we can approach the practices in a healthy way: acknowledging our tendency to misuse them, but also coming to each practice with an openness to grace and God's work within us.[4]

Practices should also reflect the uniqueness of the practitioner. A single practice doesn't always look the same. Take prayer as an example. Some people connect meaningfully with God by using prewritten prayers and others prefer to say whatever comes to mind. Some pray more easily out loud, and others prefer to pray in their minds. Some find prayer easier in groups and others in solitude. I personally know some artists who struggled with prayer until they discovered they could pray using art and beautiful images as aids. One person might excel in intercessory prayer (praying for the needs of others and the world) while another is more comfortable with contemplative or listening prayer. Prayer is a necessary discipline and habit. But it will look different for each person based on the unique way God has made them—and that's okay! Rather than force yourself into a mold, try to discover an expression of a practice that works for how God has uniquely made you.

Spending Your Time

When it comes to our use of time, it's easy to be shortsighted. Some of us are simply trying to make it through the day, and then the week, and before we know it, a month, a season, or a year has passed. Crafting your rhythm for life requires looking at time from two perspectives: regularly and seasonally. Regularly means approaching time from a daily, weekly, or monthly perspective. Seasonally means considering time from a bimonthly, quarterly, once in a while, or annual mindset.

As you consider regular or seasonal practices, get specific in setting goals. Will you do it daily, several times a week, biweekly, monthly, quarterly, once a year? For example, you might write, "Exercise three times a week for at least thirty minutes" or "read Scripture daily" or "take a two-week vacation once a year."

Growth

When integrating any new practice or discipline, it's easy to get overly ambitious. But it takes time for a habit to become an integral part of your life—anywhere from twenty-one days to nine months, depending on the researchers you ask. So, for example, if your goal is to run a triathlon but you find yourself out of breath simply from trying to get into the spandex training gear—you will need to find an easier first step. You might start with walking, then speed walking, and then jogging.

It's the same with our spiritual practices.

If you're just starting out, set an attainable goal and build on it over time. God is patient with us. The least we can do is be patient with ourselves. Anytime we take any step or movement toward God, he is elated. So, if you're just starting to build a morning routine with God, start with ten minutes: five minutes of reading Scripture and five minutes of prayer. Once you get that down, start building on it.

In the worksheets, you'll notice that there is a category for growth. That's because you can't do it all right now. The things you hope to integrate eventually can be written in the growth areas section. You might also want to look back at insights you wrote down for further learning and study and jot them in the growth areas.

From Task to Presence

When I was preparing to plant a church in Vancouver, BC, my wife and I spent six weeks of 2011 in Manhattan with the team at Redeemer City to City and a handful of other church planters. One session from there has been burned into my memory—the one in which Tim Keller outlined his own daily practices. I remember that he said, "I try not to leave my morning time of Scripture and prayer without having some sense of encountering Jesus." He reminded me of something I once read by the pastor Charles Spurgeon: "I must take care above all that I cultivate communion with Christ, for though that can never be the basis of my peace—mark that—yet it will be the channel of it."[5] All our discipline and practices are only channels that open us up to the presence of Christ our Peace. But we can get our wires crossed here.

I started meeting once a month with Araz to provide spiritual direction and discipleship. Despite having been a Christian for several decades, she struggled to connect with God in a meaningful way. There had been seasons when she faithfully used my church's version of the Daily Offices. She read Scripture, she prayed. Sometimes it was helpful. But as a project manager, she found that it all easily became a task to fulfill.

I encouraged Araz to experiment with some contemplative practices—specifically, sitting quietly with God in the morning and the Ignatian examen. I also encouraged her to meditate on smaller passages of Scripture or just one story from the Gospels at a time. I wanted her to see if there might be practices more suited for her temperament—ones that could gently counter her propensity to perform.

Don't get me wrong; sometimes we need to stretch ourselves with discipline. We don't want our practices to be dependent on whether we *feel* like doing them at a given moment. But even in our discipline, we want practices that are respectful of who God has made us to be. And I felt that Araz was trying to fit into an expression of a practice that wasn't quite the right fit for how God had made her. The shoes were a size too small and constricting her movement.

A few weeks into this process Araz told me about an experience she had at one of our Sunday worship services. We were short on Communion servers and she was asked to help. She said normally she would have declined, because she would think she needed to be more consistent with her spiritual disciplines before she served. But as she learned to discover spiritual practices that shifted from being a task to helping her experience God's presence, she felt the freedom to serve with joy because it didn't depend on her performance.

With any spiritual practice, we want to move from task to presence. The goal isn't discipline for discipline's sake. It is rather to cultivate our union with Christ and to anchor ourselves in the freedom of the gospel.

A Few Tips for Getting Started

It's possible to design a rhythm for life that is unattainable. Alternatively, you can set your sights too low. So how should you approach it?

First, consider your stage of life. Life has ebbs and flows. If you're in the middle of writing a dissertation or raising young children, you will need basic, attainable practices. But if you're in a season where you have time to spare and extra energy to spend, you may want to try new disciplines and have a fuller schedule. Most importantly, be in prayerful, reflective conversation with your community: What is God asking of you in this season?

Second, try to focus on what is essential. What are the practices, disciplines, and habits you need to really flourish in your vocation? Don't treat your rhythm like an overcrowded pantry. Think of it more like a refined, simple, nutritious, and yet remarkably pleasurable meal. Another way of looking at it is this: what are the basics that, if removed, would cause your life to start to falter? Alternatively, what practice or practices, if not added into your life, would cause you to miss out on stepping into who God has made you to be?

These are just a few questions and suggestions to keep in mind as we embark on the next part of our journey together. May your rhythm for life always help you move from task to presence.

7

Up—Upward to God

I press on toward the goal to win the prize for which
God has called me heavenward in Christ Jesus.

PHILIPPIANS 3:14

My best definition of "grace" is this: grace is not something God gives us,
but God giving himself to us. This is what changes our identity.

KLYNE SNODGRASS

THE DYING WORDS OF THE POLITICIAN Winston Churchill were, "I'm bored with it all." The last words of Steve Jobs, the innovator behind Apple, were, "Oh wow. Oh wow. Oh wow." But the last words of blues singer Bessie Smith were, "I'm going, but I'm going in the name of the Lord." My friend's father passed away abruptly after a short fight with cancer. His dying words were, "Amen."

When you reach the end of the road, what do you want to be thinking about? The drudgery of life, the awe of life, or Jesus Christ and a quiet "Amen" to all he has done?

How do we end well?

When we keep our vocation at the forefront of our minds, we are on the path to ending well. The apostle Paul modeled this well. He articulated his vocation with clarity to the urban church in the ancient city of Philippi when he said: "I want to know Christ—yes, to know the power of his resurrection and participation in his sufferings.... Forgetting what is behind and straining toward what is ahead, I press on toward the goal to win the prize for which God has called me heavenward in Christ Jesus" (Phil 3:10, 13-14). The one thing Paul wanted was to know Jesus, and his focus was quite simple: onward and upward toward Christ.

As death peered around the bend at him, Paul was able to write to his young protégé Timothy, "I have fought the good fight, I have finished the race, I have kept the faith" (2 Tim 4:7). Paul finished well. Because he structured his whole life around his "one thing" vocation. He traveled from city to city throughout the ancient world because he was called "to know him" and to make him known. And he depended on God's help to sustain him until the end.

Paul's "one thing" echoes a psalm by King David. He wrote:

One thing I ask from the LORD,
    this only do I seek:
that I may dwell in the house of the LORD
    all the days of my life,
to gaze on the beauty of the LORD. (Ps 27:4)

Although he was an imperfect and broken man, David also structured his life around this pursuit. No wonder he was described as "a man after [God's] own heart" (1 Sam 13:14). David reflected what the Danish philosopher Søren Kierkegaard called "purity of heart," which is simply to will one thing.

Before we shrink back from the shadows of spiritual giants like David or Paul, we must remember that they were ordinary people with an exceptional God. The upward rhythm is an acknowledgment that each and every follower of Jesus shares this purpose: knowing Christ on the journey onward and upward toward him.

The focus of the upward rhythm is the cultivation of our own "one thing" focus, since we can have no stable or meaningful identity or vocation apart from knowing Jesus.

Forget

The place to start in cultivating our "one thing" focus is adopting a forgetful mindset. This was Paul's approach. But this isn't a proof text to justify your poor memory (sorry not sorry). Paul advocated for a specific kind of forgetfulness: "forgetting what lies behind" (Phil 3:13). This is the same kind of forgetfulness Jesus invited when he said, "No one who puts a hand to the plow and looks back is fit for service in the kingdom of God" (Lk 9:62). If we want to live upward, we must forget "what lies behind" as we turn toward the ways of Jesus. There is no time to waste looking back.

However, Paul obviously wasn't talking about literally forgetting. What parts of the past need to be scrubbed away, erased, and forgotten? In Philippians 3, "forgetting what lies behind" comes after Paul's list of ways he could have boasted about his identity and purpose before knowing Christ: "circumcised on the eighth day, of the people of Israel, of the tribe of Benjamin, a Hebrew of Hebrews; in regard to the law, a Pharisee; as for zeal, persecuting the church; as for righteousness based on the law, faultless" (Phil 3:5-6). He had an impressive religious résumé, brushing shoulders with the elites of his day and studying with the rabbi Gamaliel (which is like saying I studied with N. T. Wright at Durham—I didn't). Before his life with Christ, Paul strove for a lot of things. He had ambitions, goals, and aspirations. He had a vision of who he wanted to be and what he wanted to accomplish. He was pious and devout. But these things were part of his misguided story. When Paul said he was "forgetting what lies behind," he meant that all these former realities were no longer the real determiners of his identity or vocation. Because now he was guided by the story of Jesus.

Adapting Saint Paul's forgetting in my own life might look like this:

> If someone else thinks they have reasons for their snobbery, check out mine. I emerged top of my class, was employed at the top advertising agency in Canada, became an award-winning

creative director, and was featured in magazines. I was defiantly of the *cooler-than-thou* tribe. As to hipsterdom—many tattoos, a Snob of Snobs in regard to culture, an Elitist; as for zeal, persecuting Comic Sans; as for righteousness based on the standards of good design, faultless.

All these details remain a part of my life story as much as the tattoo ink remains in my skin. But none of these things define me anymore. At least not in the way they once did, when they held an inappropriate importance in my sense of identity and vocation. They are no longer my core pursuit in life. And when it comes to my identity and vocation, I try to forget them entirely as I find myself in the story of Jesus.

Moving upward requires that our lives get prioritized around what really matters. Paul forgot what lay behind because he was in pursuit of something so much greater: a compelling, beautiful vision of Jesus. He forgot because the true story had come into focus.

Focus

Paul didn't just forget; he also had a goal: "I press on toward the goal to win the prize for which God has called me heavenward in Christ Jesus" (Phil 3:14). The prize he saw was knowing and gaining Christ forever. But how do we keep Jesus in focus as our one thing? What motivated Paul to press on?

He explained it plainly: "I press on to take hold of that for which Christ Jesus took hold of me" (v. 12). Life was no longer about what Paul had done or what he could achieve. He forgot about all of that. Instead, he was focused on and motivated by what Christ had done for him. "Christ Jesus took hold of me."

Knowing *whose* he was changed who Paul was. He became motivated by his identity in Christ.

When our identity is changed, our motivation is changed too. We are loved by Christ, and everything we do flows from here. There is nothing we need to do to be accepted by him. And whatever we may do for him—whatever discipline or habit we embrace—we do because we are already loved and accepted. Rather than completing a checklist of spiritual tasks, we are spurred onward and upward by the delight of God's presence. This new motivation can become the heartbeat of all our spiritual practices.

Upward Practices

The upward rhythm helps us focus on how we are growing in knowledge and love of God. There are two important types of knowing. We need to know more about God, and we can only do this by discovering how he has revealed himself through the Word. The truth about our triune God is not subjective; we don't get to determine who God is. We can only know who God is because God has first revealed himself to us. But at the same time, we need to know God in a personal and experiential way. This is subjective knowledge that comes through abiding in Christ. These two types of knowing always need to be held together. We do not want to fall into the trap of knowing a lot about God without any personal connection to our knowledge. But neither do we want to make our personal impressions and experiences the sole determiner of truth. Because we can easily deceive ourselves or settle for misperceptions of God.

As you think about upward practices, ask yourself: How do I enjoy God? What disciplines invite me to marvel at God's beauty? When in my week am I captivated by the glorious grace of Jesus Christ? The practices of the upward rhythm are simply different approaches to forgetting all the things that might distract us from God and focusing on God himself. While many practices could be highlighted, I will explore three that can serve as a baseline for your upward rhythm: solitude with God, gratitude, and sabbath.

Solitude with God. Throughout the Gospels, Jesus frequently withdraws from the busyness and demands of everyday life to be alone with God the Father (Lk 5:16). He was simply putting his own teaching into practice: "When you pray, close the door and pray to your Father, who is unseen" (Mt 6:6).

Solitude with God is a practical way to develop our "one thing" focus, and it can be practiced in a variety of ways. The two non-negotiable ingredients, though, are Scripture and prayer.

I try to start and end my day with God, and I like to use the Daily Offices in my time alone with him. The Daily Offices are morning and evening services of prayer found in the Book of Common Prayer.[1] They help me bookend my day to create a "one thing" focus. I prefer more liturgical or structured prayer because it takes the focus off of myself and my own words. It also brings in a few other practices like confession, historic prayers, and intercessory prayer for topics I wouldn't naturally think to pray for. However, I don't feel bound to prewritten prayers either. Sometimes I simply speak with Jesus and try to listen to him. Other times I try to express some of the liturgical prayers in my own words.

There are other ways to approach solitude with God.

Yui grew up as an atheist and became a follower of Jesus shortly after her first child was born. She was baptized in her thirties. A little over a decade later, she realized that she struggled to read Scripture simply because she had no desire to do it. And so she prayed a simple prayer: "Lord, please give me a desire for your Word."

God answered that prayer.

At the time, Yui was a teacher. The day after she started praying her simple prayer, she decided to arrive at school early so that she could read her Bible at her desk. When the bell rang two hours later and students started to flood into the room, she was surprised. It felt like no time at all had passed.

Ever since then, Yui has spent two hours every morning, five days a week, reading, studying, and digesting Scripture. As a teacher, her classroom provided her a quiet space away from the busyness of her home, and the practice sustained her in her work. Now that she's retired, she enjoys walking to her favorite coffee shop to spend her morning there.

Yui uses a Bible reading plan so she can read the whole Bible every year. She also buys the occasional devotional or commentary to help her go deeper into specific books of the Bible. But time and a Bible are the two core ingredients to her practice, along with brief prayers. Of course, two hours is more than the average person may be able to carve out in their schedule. I only share her story to encourage you to ask God for the hunger to know him through his Word, especially if the desire is weak.

Anna has a less cognitive and more contemplative approach to her solitude with God. She begins her morning with prayer and meditation. First she centers her mind and heart on God's Word using the Sacred Space app, which provides a brief reflective guide on a small portion of Scripture. Then she spends some time in prayer, reciting a few affirmations she developed for herself that express her values and vocation and help her keep what matters with God in focus: "Grace. Joy. Purpose." After that, Anna prays for people who come to mind—people she may want to connect with or who are going through something and have asked for prayer. She simply names them before God. Finally, she practices centering prayer. She listens and waits.

This might sound like a lot, but it only takes her about thirty minutes each morning, and these are the expressions of solitude that help Anna connect with God.

When it comes to solitude with God, there are two principles that you must apply: set aside time, and find a place.

You need to set aside time. Time is our most valuable "possession." We're all busy and want to maximize our time. The most helpful thing to do is to guard a specific block of time in your day. But also resist the urge to think that more time equals deeper spirituality.

Quality is always more important than quantity when it comes to solitude with God. And yet, developing a routine of quality solitude often leads to a desire to have more and more—and so the quantity increases. You can start small (for example, fifteen minutes every morning and evening) and let God grow that time with you and for you. But fight for this time in your daily schedule.

It also helps to have a specific place. The Gospels highlight how Jesus routinely went to a solitary place and prayed. I suggest that you find your own solitary place where you are free from distractions and won't be interrupted, so that you can focus on connecting with God through prayer and sacred readings. During the rainy season in Vancouver, I have a chair in my bedroom that I only sit in for my solitude with God. However, when the weather improves, I often do my morning devotionals in a quiet place outside in the city. It helps me feel connected to God and his purposes for the world. Yui's place was her classroom and now a coffee shop, and Anna's place is her home before her family wakes up. Find your place!

Just as it's important to have daily or almost daily solitude with God, it can be helpful to carve out times of extended solitude. I know people who set aside one afternoon per week, one day per month, and one weekend per year. While others are more disciplined on this front than I am, from time to time I have intentionally sought these longer periods of solitude with God.

When I was offered my first job in ministry, I set aside two days to be alone with God and booked a room at a local retreat center. My wife and I share a car, however, and she needed it for work. I thought about the role of walking in spiritual pilgrimages like the Camino de Santiago and decided that a sixteen-mile walk could be part of connecting with God. It turns out it was. I felt a strong sense of the Spirit's presence with me each step of the way. In fact, it was while I was walking that I discerned the answer I was seeking: a resolute "yes" to accepting the job as a gift. But when I arrived at the retreat center, I had massive blisters on my feet. Those too ended up being part of the discernment. I felt God quietly whisper to me, "Ministry will hurt. Discipleship is costly, so rest up!"

These moments of extended solitude are more seasonal than frequent for me. Sometimes people schedule them in regularly, and other times they happen in response to new opportunities or to seek God's voice for a situation. But if you pursue them at all, they are a helpful way to keep moving upward toward God.

The aim of solitude, whenever and however we practice it, is to connect in a meaningful and real way with God and to keep our focus on the upward prize of knowing him.

Brainstorm: What could solitude with God look like for you?

Gratitude. Did you know that some of the most repeated commands in Scripture are to "praise the Lord," "rejoice," and "give thanks"? Gratitude isn't a suggestion. It is a key instrument in the melody of God's ways.

Researcher Robert Emmons has proven that gratitude "is literally one of the few things that can measurably change people's lives."[2] Which is to say that even if you're not feeling thankful, choosing to practice gratitude can actually make you feel grateful and even happier. The science says so. And it's not surprising, because God commands gratitude for our flourishing.

Regular practices of gratitude are another essential ingredient in the upward rhythm because they help us sustain a grace-filled worldview. As Emmons puts it, gratitude is "a deep and abiding recognition and acknowledgment that goodness exists under even the worst life offers," and, more profoundly, "gratitude enables us to be fully human."[3] Practices of gratitude help us move away from focusing on ourselves and focus on the Giver of every good gift. And Emmons's research demonstrated that gratitude doesn't even need to be a daily practice to rewire us; a few times a week is enough (although daily is ideal)!

Gratitude can be practiced in a variety of ways.

I discovered the practice of gratitude in a prolonged season of depression, at a time when I was feeling more ungrateful than grateful. Previously I had approached gratitude as a more ad hoc practice; it wasn't intentional. I decided to dive in and bought a five-year journal.[4] Each page is devoted to one day of the year and subdivided into five sections, one for each year. I love this because as time goes by, past entries can be read as new ones are written.

At the end of each day (or most days), I write in this gratitude journal. At first I would write down basic things I was thankful for, such as my daughters' smiles, a good night's sleep, or time spent with a friend. On darker days, all I could muster were bullet-point lists of things like toothpaste, oxygen, and a home. But over the years the practice has deepened. I try to identify and give thanks for specific moments of God's presence and joy in my day.

Now that I've used this journal for a few years, I find that I feel gratitude and joy all over again as I read previous entries. For example, here is what I have written for September 9:

> 2016—Two opportunities to share faith. My mom being in town. Your Spirit going ahead of me. Maggie taking some of her first steps. Colin being in town.

> 2017—Daddy and daughters' day while Julia had the day to herself. Jon in town. Premarital with Julie and Steven. The truth that you always pursue us. Time with Alida and her new boyfriend. Swinging Maggie by her hands and feet and her repeating, "Do it again!"

2018—"Although we are weeping help us keep sowing, the seeds of your kingdom for the day of your reaping" made me cry during worship. Sarah's prophetic image of a woman's arm around my back providing comfort—immediately thought of Julia and my counselor. A day of prayer answered for encouragement through Don, Gogo, and Paul.

2019—The joy of gospel partnership with Preston. A little bit of progress on Rhythms for Life revisions. Ansley's first soccer practice and fun as a family.

Gratitude draws me closer to the generous heart of God. It's changed me. I have become a more joyous person and less afraid of painful moments.

As part of her morning meditation routine, Anna (from above) also includes prayers of gratitude. She starts her day by identifying and naming all that she is grateful for: breath, her home, her family, the knowledge of God, and anything else that comes to mind. She simply names each one quietly before God. She also gives thanks for what is to come in the day ahead, whether work, a meeting that is scheduled, or anticipating returning home to her family. The practice of gratitude is just as effective without pen and paper.

Once when I was speaking at a small conference with my psychologist friend Hillary, she guided people through a basic gratitude exercise developed by Dr. Rick Hanson.[5] Hanson suggests that you sit in a quiet place, close your eyes, and focus on a positive moment from your day. As you do, pay attention to your body. When you think of your positive moment, do you feel it anywhere in your body? Can you imagine it physically? For example, if your heart feels full, try to imagine it full of white light and let the light grow and expand. If your stomach feels warm, identify it with a color (like blue) and let the color spread and grow. Try to spend a minute or two with the memory.

It was amazing to be in the room as Hillary took people through this exercise. A palpable change took place. The feeling of the room was so different afterward—everything felt calm. If you try this practice, finish by thanking God for the moment you thought about and for how powerful our recollection of such memories can be.

Another friend, Michele, has found that most of her gratitude flows from meditating on what Jesus has accomplished for her on the cross. Saint Ignatius used to instruct his disciples to imagine Jesus crucified, and then to pray. Reflecting on the cross through Scripture or meditation is a surefire way to cultivate thankfulness.

Gratitude can be practiced and expressed in many ways. But no matter how you may choose to do it, the ultimate goal is to move our attention away from ourselves and upward toward God with thankfulness, rejoicing, and praise.

Brainstorm: What could gratitude look like for you?

Sabbath. You cannot flourish as a person if you do not rest. Western culture is biased toward busyness, accomplishment, and completing to-do lists. There is a place for this in our lives within moderation. But we were primarily made to enjoy God and his creation, and the pinnacle of his creation is rest.

The Sabbath (or Shabbat) was historically practiced within Judaism from sundown on Friday until sundown on Saturday. This time period represents the seventh day of creation when God rested and declared it holy (Gen 2:1-3). However, the New Testament does not prescribe a specific day. By the fourth century it had become the norm for Christians to practice sabbath or "the Lord's Day" on Sundays. Some say this represents the first day of the week and the advent of new creation in Christ; others say it represents the third day of resurrection. Whatever the rationale, I find Ross Lockhart's definition of sabbath helpful: it is "a commitment to regular worship with the church family; a desire to engage practices that recreate and restore body, mind, and spirit; and a curiosity to explore the power of prayer."[6] Peter Scazzero similarly defines it as "a twenty-four-hour period in which we stop work, enjoy rest, practice delight, and contemplate God."[7]

Most followers of Jesus will make Sundays their sabbath. This way, you can prioritize being present and engaged in Sunday worship at your church. However, you'll need to consider your schedule when you pick your day. No matter what, you need a twenty-four-hour period of rest, because it is part of the fabric of all creation, including you. And each God-honoring sabbath can be marked by the following three qualities: it promotes life, it's restorative, and it's worshipful.

First, sabbath promotes life. In Scripture, Jesus healed on the Sabbath, even though the religious leaders of his day opposed it. Why? Because sabbath is about life. What you do on a sabbath day can vary, but the question is, "Does it bring life?" This isn't the same as, "Does it make me feel good?" Rather, it's about asking if what you're doing is for your flourishing. For example, although binge-watching Netflix might be enjoyable and relaxing, it is not a practice that anchors you in the abundant life Jesus came to give. Perhaps try a short walk, sitting quietly, or taking a nap. Many people find it helpful to stay away from technology and screens altogether for one day a week. (I offer more practical boundaries around technology and devices in chapter eight under stewardship.)

Second, sabbath is restorative. If you're limping into every sabbath, your entire schedule likely needs to be reevaluated. Sabbath is not solely a time to recover from a busy week. It is a time to be rejuvenated by abiding in God's rest.

Third, sabbath is worshipful. God didn't ordain sabbath so that we could indulge in our interests and pleasures. Let's be honest: we already do that enough in the week. Sabbath is a time to enjoy God and seek his presence in quiet, slow, abiding ways. It's a time to delight in who God is through practices that help us connect with him. This is why Sunday worship is so important. God designed us to flourish as we worship him with others. Although our faith is deeply personal, it shouldn't be privatized. We need to be part of a worshiping community.

You may think you have a good reason to skip the practice of sabbath, but there really is no legitimate excuse. Many people— some who are busier than you—keep it faithfully. It's a matter of priority, not busyness. In Scripture, God's people often failed to keep the Sabbath. In a season where this was the case, he made a profoundly beautiful promise to his people:

> If you keep your feet from breaking the Sabbath,
>   from doing as you please on my holy day,
> if you call the Sabbath a delight
>   and the LORD's holy day honorable;
> and if you honor it by not going your own way,
>   and not doing as you please or speaking idle words,
> then you will find your joy in the LORD,
>   and I will cause you to ride in triumph on the heights of
>   the land. (Is 58:13-14)

This is why the author Jacqueline Lapsley writes, "One does not derive happiness from Sabbath observance unless one already understands it to be a gift that produces happiness."[8]

I share more about my own sabbath practice in chapter nine, on the withward rhythm. But as you think about sabbath, remember that it is a practice that helps us keep our lives and time structured around God and the deeper order of all creation. And for this reason, it keeps us moving upward, because the sabbath now is just a taste of the sabbath rest that is to come (Heb 4).

Brainstorm: What could sabbath look like for you?

Ending Well

We don't know when our last day will be. This is why the psalmist prays, "Teach us to number our days, / that we may gain a heart of wisdom" (Ps 90:12). When we keep in mind that our days are numbered, we can live wisely. The writer Annie Dillard famously said, "How we spend our days is, of course, how we spend our lives."[9]

If you live upward today, and tomorrow, and the next day—you're on the narrow path of grace. You will be filling your days and ultimately your life with the only thing that matters and lasts: Jesus Christ, who has made us his own. You will end well.

May the practices of your upward rhythm help you forget and focus on the upward prize of knowing Christ forever.

Up—God: Examples

This is my current upward rhythm. Please keep in mind that vocationally I am a pastor.

Regular

- Every morning at eight o'clock, thirty minutes of solitude with God using Morning Office
- Almost every evening at ten o'clock, twenty minutes of solitude with God using Evening Office or Ignatian examen
- Almost every day, gratitude journal
- Sabbath from Friday sundown to Saturday sundown
- One-to-three times a week, fifteen minutes of journaling
- Two weekly four-hour blocks for study not related to preaching
- Weekly Sunday worship

Seasonal

- Extended time of solitude two-to-four times a year
- Read one book a month that cultivates my love for God and not just my knowledge

- Meaningfully engage in the church calendar (Advent through Trinity Sunday) and discern seasonal practices

Growth

- Learn more about the role of joy in the mission of God

This is Michele's upward rhythm. She is the primary caregiver for two toddlers and also works part-time.

Regular

- Most mornings, fifteen minutes of solitude with God in the sunroom (currently using a devotional guide)
- Drive on workdays: Christian podcast, worship music, or quiet to pray
- Evenings: (1) kids' routine of story Bible and short prayers and (2) short prayers and sharing grateful moments in bed with husband
- One one-to-two-hour block a week to pray, study Scripture, and journal
- Sabbath on Sundays (worship at church, quiet time with family in the afternoon)

Seasonal

- Participate in annual women's retreat
- Fast once or twice a year for a day or two
- Get out into nature and praise God

Growth

- Learn more about God as Father and what it means for me to be adopted

UP—GOD
Worksheet

Regular

Seasonal

Growth

8

In—Inward to Self

*We all, who with unveiled faces contemplate the Lord's glory, are
being transformed into his image with ever-increasing glory.*

2 CORINTHIANS 3:18

*The more we get what we now call "ourselves" out of the way and
let God take us over, the more truly ourselves we become.*

C. S. LEWIS

IN 1954 GRAHAM SUTHERLAND WAS COMMISSIONED to paint a
portrait of Winston Churchill, the prime minister who led England
through World War II. Upon its completion, the first person to see
the portrait was Churchill's wife, Clementine. Reports say she quite
liked its realism.

However, when the portrait was presented to Churchill, his re-
action was different. He was deeply upset and decried the painting
as "filthy." He took a violent dislike toward it.

Eventually Clementine had the painting destroyed.[1] (The artist
in me grieves for poor Graham Sutherland.)

Churchill saw an uncanny portrait of himself, and it was
jarring and uncomfortable. But he refused to be forced out of the
house of mirrors. Although others felt the portrait was accurate,

Churchill preferred the less authentic picture of himself that he held in his mind.

What if a portrait was painted of you? But what if this portrait was not only accurate physically, but also unveiled everything hidden within yourself—all the things you filter out and hide? Would you ever want to see that portrait? It would be the authentic you.

Like Churchill, we prefer to live with a distorted view of ourselves. We hold on to illusion rather than raw truth. Psychologists have demonstrated this in numerous studies. We exaggerate our best features and diminish our worst. We stretch out and amplify everything we like about ourselves or wish to see in ourselves. We find our best angle under the right lighting. We hold up our brightest moments as our "true selves." No wonder it is so easy to buy into the cultural story that we're all good people deep down. We're wired to do so.

Turning our attention toward ourselves for the purpose of self-examination isn't easy. We prefer illusions of ourselves. But it's also difficult because it can be hard to understand ourselves. Saint Augustine wrote, "I find my own self hard to grasp."[2] He was in good company with Saint Basil, who said, "We are more likely to understand the heavens than ourselves."[3] Although I am well aware that I'm a finite creature, when I look within, I can feel like I'm peering into the darkness of a bottomless well. My "authentic self" is nowhere to be found.

Moreover, the inward journey is sometimes met with suspicion or even discouraged altogether. Sometimes I'm skeptical toward it too. It is possible to pay too much attention to ourselves, especially in our image-driven age of selfies and social media. Too much introspection can become narcissistic. But this doesn't mean we should run in the opposite direction and ignore self-examination.

Christianity is unashamedly a religion of the heart: the entirety of our inner lives. And Scripture speaks of our innermost self. David declared to God in prayer, "Yet you desired faithfulness even in the womb; / you taught me wisdom in that secret place" (Ps 51:6). The apostle Paul rejoiced that even though our physical bodies slowly decay, "inwardly we are being renewed day by day" (2 Cor 4:16). Jesus expressed deep concern for our heart—the center of who we are (Mk 7:14-23). It's from the heart that sin originates and it is from within that Christ begins our transformation. As Paul asked, "Do you not realize that Christ Jesus is in you?" (2 Cor 13:5).

The inward rhythm is not a call to discover ourselves in ourselves. There is not some true version of yourself buried deep within you that you have yet to unearth. Rather, "your life is now hidden with Christ in God" (Col 3:3). The inward rhythm is about discovering ourselves in Christ by discovering him within ourselves. This may feel a bit like mental gymnastics, but it is the beautiful mystery of Christian inner life. This rhythm embraces practices to learn how to behold Jesus in our innermost being as we discover our hidden life in him.

Our Whole Selves

If you're hesitant about the inward journey, we can likely agree on this point: we cannot know ourselves apart from God.

God reveals his identity as the triune God so that we can know who we are. But have you thought about it the other way? We cannot know God apart from ourselves either. John Calvin grasped this point, explaining, "Without knowledge of self there is no knowledge of God. Without knowledge of God there is no knowledge of self."[4] As we know more about God we discover more about ourselves. And as we learn more about ourselves we can also discover more about God.

If we know a lot about God but do not know him within the depths of who we are, God might only be an idea or abstraction. Yet if we focus exclusively on ourselves without looking to God to reveal who we are, we will inevitably settle for self-authorship and misguided stories. We will have a distorted view of ourselves. We need to know God in ourselves and know ourselves in God. A healthy approach to the inner life is neither obsessed with nor neglectful of ourselves.

There are three things we immediately learn about ourselves in light of the story of God: we were made in his image, we were declared very good, and shortly thereafter we fell into sin (see Gen 1–3). Any genuine self-examination must come to terms with the fact that we are not merely imperfect or broken. We are not just people who happen to sin. We are sinners. And our sin is never contained to just one part of our lives. Klyne Snodgrass practically grabs us by the shoulders to shake us awake when he says that sin is "the propensity to self-centeredness and worse, is not a tenth factor of identity but a reality that pervades all our identity."[5] Sin's pervasiveness causes us to misuse spiritual gifts, boast in talents, seek misaligned values, and live for idolatrous purposes.

So . . . what are we supposed to do with our sin?

We accept it.

This probably isn't the advice you're used to hearing about sin. But I don't mean we should just get over the fact that sin is part and parcel of what it means to be human. This is not a "stop worrying about it because it's not really that big of a deal" mentality. Nor am I saying we should cast ourselves headlong toward the mantra of the serpent, "Do what thou shalt wilt."[6]

What I am saying is that we must accept our sin before we can do anything else with it. I can hear you protesting. Scripture seems to advocate a different approach: our sin nature must be crucified (Lk 9:23-24; Rom 8:13; Gal 5:24)! But think about it: we cannot crucify something we deny.

I will never forget the day I read these words by psychologist David Benner. They were a game changer for me, inducing the type of aha moment that seems to slow down time so that everything stands still. He says:

Scriptures seem clear enough about the importance of cruci-
fying our sin nature. But attempts to eliminate things that we
find in our self that we do not first accept as part of us rely on
denial, not crucifixion. Crucifixion should be directed toward
our sin nature. And we must first accept it as *our* nature, not
simply human nature.[7]

Let those words sink in deeply.

The inward journey is not merely embracing our good parts and
ignoring our bad parts. Nor is it compulsively identifying our sin
to the neglect of any good in us. Instead of embracing ourselves
selectively, Christian self-acceptance embraces the whole picture
of who we are.

We can do this because God doesn't shrink back from our
failures and mistakes, our sins and transgressions. He always moves
toward us, even the darkest parts of us, with love. As Paul wrote,
"God demonstrates his own love for us in this: While we were still
sinners, Christ died for us" (Rom 5:8). In accepting our whole
selves before God, we embrace that we are not just sinners; we are
beloved sinners.

This makes all the difference.

Grace allows us to muster the courage to stand before our true
self-portrait, no matter how disturbing, ugly, broken, and sinful, and
accept it as authentic.

Far too often we try to crucify ourselves. We don't use nails
though. We hammer ourselves with self-hatred. But nobody has ever
hated themselves into being a better person. Brennan Manning describes our sin nature as "the imposter." He advocates for a surprising
approach toward this part of ourselves. "The imposter must be called
out of hiding, accepted, and embraced," writes Manning. "We make
friends with the imposter and accept that we are impoverished and
broken."[8] Hatred is not what paved the way to the cross. The hatred
in the hearts of others may have crucified Jesus. But love is why

Christ was crucified. Love paved the way to the cross, endured the cross, and brought life through the cross.

We crucify our sin, but not with self-hatred. We crucify our sin with the love of Christ.

Becoming Ourselves

Self-acceptance isn't the end goal. As we embrace our whole selves, Scripture invites us to identify our "old self" and "new self." Some authors describe this as the "false self" and "true self," or the "pretend self" and "actual self." We bring our old self before Christ to experience grace, redemption, forgiveness, death, and resurrection, because accepting ourselves doesn't mean excusing or justifying these old and sinful parts. We bring every part of ourselves to Jesus. And in this process, we receive the gift of our new self in Christ. We are becoming ourselves before God.

But this is also not about self-authorship. We do not become our new selves by picking and choosing which characteristics of ours we like best. Rather, we become who we are in Christ by fixing our attention and hearts on him. The apostle Paul wrote to the church in Corinth, "We all, who with unveiled faces contemplate the Lord's glory, are being transformed into his image with ever-increasing glory" (2 Cor 3:18). God's glory rubs off on us—and when it does, we become the most authentic version of ourselves.

The word Paul uses for "contemplate" here means "to behold," as in, to look at something in a mirror. As we learn about Jesus and grow in our knowledge of him, he becomes our own reflection. But as we start to take on his likeness, we are not erased or eradicated. We don't become a mindless drone or soulless clone. C. S. Lewis, one of the greatest storytellers of the twentieth century, put it this way:

> The more we get what we now call "ourselves" out of the way and let Him take us over, the more truly ourselves we become. There is so much of Him that millions and millions of "little Christs,"

all different, will still be too few to express Him fully. . . . It is when I turn to Christ, when I give myself up to His Personality, that I first begin to have a real personality of my own.[9]

There is something so beautiful about becoming ourselves in Christ. We're already seen and known by him. And even if we don't fully understand ourselves, Jesus does. As he walks with us, he calls who he sees and knows into existence.

Inward Practices

The *inward* rhythm helps us focus on beholding Jesus in our innermost being. It's a movement toward our identity in Christ, discerning and expressing our spiritual gifts, discerning and living in alignment with our values, and fulfilling our personal vocation. As you think about inward practices, ask yourself: Who am I in Christ? What disciplines and practices invite me to accept my whole self? When in my week am I able to slow down and dwell in Christ's abiding presence? The practices of the inward rhythm are different approaches to accepting our whole selves as we become ourselves in Christ. In this chapter we'll explore self-examination, stewardship, and spiritual guidance.

Self-examination. I use the Daily Offices as part of my solitude with Christ. But I also keep a journal by my side (in addition to my gratitude journal). I have journaled (off and on) for most of my Christian life.

My journal helps me focus on God and prayer, as I'm prone to a wandering mind. And I like to use two different-colored pens to record different things. I use black when I write out my own prayers. When I record my impressions about a Scripture that has struck me, or feel a sense of God's presence, I use red. Over the years, the red-pen entries have helped me learn how to discern God's voice. They are impressions I can reflect on and pray about with trusted friends. And, looking back at my entries over the years, I can see when I was correct in discerning God's voice and when I may have missed the mark. The red pen just makes it easier to reidentify these moments (they aren't *Thus saith the Lord!* to me).

My journal is also a place for self-examination. It's easy for me to get disconnected from my heart. I can be slow to name my feelings. Sitting down with my journal helps me reconnect with myself.

Since it can be easy to get lost in introspection, I have tried to model my journal after the Psalms. Once I've explored a thought or struggle in detail, I take a break from myself. I write *Selah*. No one is entirely sure what *Selah* means in the Psalms, but it typically denotes a change of focus. The psalmist may be lamenting or naming a frustration before God, but then *Selah* appears, and the poet moves from his own circumstances to God's character (see Ps 3 as an example). So after my *Selah,* I write as much as I can about God's character and goodness. I spend time praising God even if I don't feel like it. I might write *Selah* once again and return to some more self-exploration and self-examination. But *Selah* for me is a way to keep that balance between God and the self that Calvin advocates.

Keeping a journal may not be your thing. A less cognitive and more contemplate practice worth your consideration is the daily examen.[10] In his now classic work, *Spiritual Exercises*, Ignatius Loyola encourages the examen. It's a simple five-step process that is sometimes described as praying backward through your day:

1. Become aware of God's presence.

2. Review the day with gratitude.

3. Pay attention to your emotions.

4. Choose one feature of the day and pray from it.

5. Look forward to tomorrow.

My friend Valerie works in the exhausting yet rewarding world of social work. At the end of a long day, she pours a cup of tea, sits in a chair, and brings her attention to God. "I am with you always, to the end of the age," she repeats to herself. This promise from Matthew 28:20 helps her become aware of God's presence. "You are with me, Lord," she prays.

Valerie then starts to review her day with gratitude. She's thankful she had a good night's sleep the evening before. She is grateful for her roommate. She enjoyed the small-roast quality coffee they shared before rushing out the door. She's thankful to have a car and a job and for her coworkers who help her stay grounded.

As Valerie pays attention to her emotions, she realizes she's feeling burdened and sad. She grieves for a young girl she'd met who had been removed from her parents. She stays with this moment from her day and the weightiness. And she prays, "Lord, have mercy." She also gives thanks for the people who are trying their best to help the girl find a temporary home, and prays for her parents to get the help they need, "Lord, have mercy." Valerie takes the last sip of her tea and says, "Goodnight, Lord. See you in the morning."

Sometimes Valerie practices the examen on the drive home from work rather than before bed, or even on a run. People typically do it in the evening, but it can also be done during the morning or your lunch break. Some people prefer to do the examen in these earlier times of the day, as it helps them see their previous day less critically and with a more gracious perspective. Similar to your practice of solitude, you might set aside a specific time and place to do this. Typically, a meaningful examen takes about fifteen minutes. However, self-examination doesn't need to take place on a daily basis. For some, once a week is enough.

The examen, whenever you choose to practice it, is a way of re-living your day with Christ. Like a family discussion of the day at the dinner table, Jesus wants much more than an aloof "good" to the question, "How was your day?" He wants to reflect on it with you because he wants to be present with *you*. And Jesus wants to reveal how he has been present to you even if you didn't see it throughout the day. As you get accustomed to the examen, it becomes easier to identify God in your ordinary life, as well as when you are aligned or misaligned with the values of his kingdom.

Alternatively, Aaron works through the Great Litany in the Book of Common Prayer once a week. The Litany is a structured way to examine our sin from a variety of angles and to seek God's mercy. Anglicans typically ask God to forgive "the things we've done and left undone." The Great Litany helps Aaron consider his own blind spots and identify what he may have left undone—or what he may have done and not even realized. Here are a few of the prayers from it:

> From all blindness of heart; from pride, vainglory,
> and hypocrisy; from envy, hatred, and malice; and from all want
> of charity,
> *Good Lord, deliver us.*

> From all inordinate and sinful affections; and from all the
> deceits of the world, the flesh, and the devil,
> *Good Lord, deliver us.*

> From all false doctrine, heresy, and schism; from hardness
> of heart, and contempt of thy Word and commandment,
> *Good Lord, deliver us.*[11]

Whatever expressions of self-examination you choose, the practice can help you move inward toward your whole self before Christ.

Brainstorm: What could self-examination look like for you?

Stewardship. Although stewardship is related to self-examination, I want to treat it as its own practice, because the way we steward what God has entrusted us unveils a lot about ourselves.

I structured my church's Community Groups around the four rhythms: up, in, with, and out. In the early days, the inward rhythm involved having our groups, which were typically composed of twelve-to-fifteen people, break into smaller groups of three-to-four for one of their meetings in a month. As these smaller groups practiced the inward rhythm, they were encouraged to explore five topics: finances, relationships, sin, time, and work. But over the years we found that these topics simply became checklists: Are my finances in order? Check. Are my relationships healthy? Yes. Is there any active sin in my life? Check. But a checklist mentality stops short of true stewardship.

God wants us to steward our finances, relationships, purity, time, and work. But stewardship isn't just about doing the right things. It includes examining how we *relate* to what has been entrusted to us. For example, your finances might be in order: you might spend wisely, your savings may be growing, your investments might be performing well, and you could even give generously. But money could still have an inordinate grip on your heart. Taking time to examine your heart related to money might help you see that you are still building your trust on your wealth rather than Jesus.

Reflecting on what has been entrusted to us is an opportunity to discover more about ourselves. And once again, as we see ourselves more fully, we must ask ourselves: Can we accept the honest picture?

I was struck by a practice of stewardship described by the Austrian designer Stefan Sagmeister in his documentary *The Happy Film.* Once a week, he evaluates how well he has embodied his own values. He says, "What I normally do on Monday mornings is a weekly rating. I've been doing it for years and years. It's basically twelve things that I'm going to change about myself. A one means I've been really, really good. Whereas a five means I've been really, really bad."[12] Sagmeister's list includes things like don't drink alcohol, have more guts, help somebody, do something with my friends, and be more flexible. He tallies up his total score and divides it by twelve, and that's his rating for the week.

I can't advocate that you start rating yourself this way. God does not want you to attribute a grade or score to your performance in personal growth. However, the intentionality Sagmeister brings to assessing his week within the context of his values is a good practice. It is a form of stewardship to ask, "Is my life moving toward the values of the kingdom? Am I growing in virtue?" You might take a little time once a week to review your values. Have you been aligned with the kingdom? Is the "shadow side" of any of your values wreaking havoc? This is another angle to self-examination and to stewarding our lives well.

An overlooked dimension of stewardship is self-care. Some people get nervous the moment we talk about taking care of ourselves because they've mistaken modern workaholism for faithfulness. But God has entrusted our bodies and souls to us to be stewarded. And stewardship of our bodies does not mean endless productivity, nor does it mean endless navel gazing. I've heard people quote 1 Timothy 4:8—"For physical training is of some value, but godliness has value for all things, holding promise for both the present life and the life to come"—as a way to justify their neglect of their bodies. But this isn't what Paul had in mind. He is only stressing that godliness is of greater significance. And he acknowledges there is some value to physical training because we are embodied creatures.

There is still one more critical area of stewardship to explore. In our technological age, we must consider how we relate to our devices. If you are among the average person who checks their phone roughly every ten minutes (which means looking at your phone eighty times a day), then developing some patterns of stewardship to limit your use of technology will be important.[13] In his book *The Common Rule*, Justin Earley suggests a variety of habits, such as turning to Scripture before your phone in the morning and even shutting your phone down for an hour every day. He also suggests intentionally curating your consumption of media. Limit it to 4 hours a week (and one hour at a time)—whether that's news, articles, short clips, or movies. Often on my Sabbath, I take the SIM card out of my smartphone and use a "dumb" phone that can only call and text. This keeps me off social media and stops me from impulsively checking my email. Whatever you may do, what boundaries will help you use technology in a healthy way?

As you think about stewardship ask yourself, what patterns of exercise and rest do I need in order to flourish in my pursuit of godliness?

It may be helpful to reflect on your stewardship once a week or once a month. And while you can do this on your own, it is always helpful to do it with someone else who may ask you the questions you don't want to ask yourself. The goal is not to just be good at stewardship but to be a good steward: rightly handling and relating to what has been entrusted to us.

Brainstorm: What could stewardship look like for you?

Guidance. We tend to think that we know ourselves best. But this isn't the truth. We are only entirely known by God. And we discover who we are in relationship with others. We need others to help us discern if we are stewarding our lives in a way that honors God. We'll explore spiritual friendships under the "with" rhythm, but I want to consider other types of relationships here that can aid us on the inward journey.

Preston meets with a spiritual director on a monthly basis. A spiritual director is trained to act as a guide for people in their spiritual journey, helping them pay attention to where God is working in their life.

When Preston began spiritual direction, he was unsure about the practice. It took a couple of months for him to settle in and trust that God would show up in the sessions. Over time, it has become a space Preston counts on for his spiritual health. Now that trust has been built with his spiritual director, Preston gets excited to enter this space and have someone listen deeply to him and to the Spirit, and help him hear how God is speaking to him. As someone who works in ministry, this is an especially important practice for Preston, because he is rarely in a conversation about God where he simply receives care.

Sometimes, Preston brings up specific situations in his life or family that he needs to process. Other times he doesn't know what exactly to talk about, and his spiritual director guides him through times of quiet and meditation on Christ to see where the invitation of the Spirit is that day. His director has helped him to see and know God's presence in his everyday life, such as in parenting and family life, and to grow in engaging confidently and compassionately with his coworkers. More than anything, Preston's practice of meeting for spiritual direction reinforces to him the truth that God is at work in his life, and that the Holy Spirit is close and does have words of life and truth to speak to him—he only needs to slow down and accept the invitation to hear them.

Similarly, once a month Katherine meets up with two other women in her "soul trio" for group spiritual direction, which their church provided some basic training on. Although the other two in her trio aren't people she sees on a regular basis, or even outside of these meetings, they have become faithful guides. This monthly gathering has been a steady rhythm in Katherine's life.

Over the years I've seen how the Enneagram, Myers-Briggs, and StrengthsFinder (among others) can be helpful guides on the journey inward. I am the personality type that doesn't like personality paradigms (if that makes me an ENFJ or a Three wing Four, so be it!), but I can't deny that they can help us examine ourselves and come to a better understanding of how our unique personalities factor into our pursuit of God. If you've never engaged in one of these paradigms, I would recommend trying one to see if it helps you see yourself in a new light.

Seasonally I have engaged in counseling—sometimes weekly, other times bimonthly or monthly. A well-trained, spiritually grounded, theologically sound counselor has been essential to my self-examination and to discovering Christ in the parts of myself that I struggle to accept. If self-acceptance has ever been hard for you, or if you've had a mental health challenge or experienced trauma, I would encourage you to visit a counselor who can become a guide on your journey inward.

Once a month, Aaron meets with one of his mentors for confession and forgiveness. While confession between friends is a somewhat common activity for most evangelicals, extending forgiveness on behalf of God is not as regular. But this scripturally mandated (and, yes, vulnerable) act of sharing our sins and failures with another person and hearing them declare God's promises of forgiveness and redemption is a powerful and healing act (see Jn 20:23)—one that can help us discover Christ with us through the presence of another in our weaknesses and sins.

The practice of receiving guidance from others helps us see ourselves in a new light and see what Jesus is up to in our inmost being.

Brainstorm: What could guidance look like for you?

Our Self-Portrait

The Catholic priest Henri Nouwen was a prolific author. One of his most beloved and widely recognized books is *The Return of the*

Prodigal Son.[14] It is a collection of his own meditations on this famous parable in Luke 15, and especially on the magnificent oil painting *The Return of the Prodigal Son* by Rembrandt. The painting had been on Nouwen's heart and mind for three years before he had the opportunity to sit privately with the original painting at the Hermitage Museum in Saint Petersburg, Russia. He wrote:

> I was stunned by its majestic beauty. Its size, larger than life; its abundant reds, browns and yellows; its shadowy recesses and bright foreground, but most of all the light-enveloped embrace of father and son surrounded by four mysterious bystanders, all gripped me with an intensity far beyond my anticipation. . . . Coming here was indeed a homecoming.[15]

The strength and tenderness of the father's hands on the back of the youngest son were one of the things that particularly moved him. He appreciated how "his outstretched hands are not begging, grasping, demanding, warning, judging, or condemning. They are hands that only bless, giving all and expecting nothing."[16] Nouwen came to see in a new way how the embrace of the Father's hands has the power to change our sense of self.

"When I look through God's eyes at my lost self and discover God's joy at my coming home," he said, "then my life may become less anguished and more trusting."[17] We discover ourselves in the Father's love showered on us in Christ. We discover our vocation in being embraced as beloved sinners. Nouwen concluded, "I now see that the hands that forgive, console, heal, and offer a festive meal must become my own."[18] We become ourselves as we reflect the nature of God into the world. This is our deepest vocation. Our truest portrait.

May the practices of your inward rhythm help you discover yourself in Christ.

In—Self: Examples

This is my current inward rhythm.

Regular

- Journal one-to-three times a week

- Examen at least once a week

- Counseling two times a month (stewardship)

- Exercise for mental health one-to-three times a week (stewardship)

- Confession with close friend/wife as needed

Seasonal

- Annual reflection/self-examination for past year

- Annual summer vacation/unplug (stewardship)

Growth

- Explore more about my Enneagram profile

This is Dianne's inward rhythm. She lives with a roommate and works full-time while completing a degree in the evening.

Regular

- Weekly counseling

- Intentional confession once a week with a friend

- Run three-to-five times a week (stewardship)

Seasonal

- Meet with spiritual director

- Meet with psychologist/physician for mental health plan

Growth

- Learn more about coping with anxiety

IN—SELF
Worksheet

Regular

Seasonal

Growth

With—Withward in Community

Let us consider how we may spur one another on toward love and good deeds, not giving up meeting together, as some are in the habit of doing, but encouraging one another—and all the more as you see the Day approaching.

HEBREWS 10:24-25

The physical presence of other Christians is a source of incomparable joy and strength to the believer.

DIETRICH BONHOEFFER

WHEN I FIRST BECAME A FOLLOWER OF JESUS, I didn't know my left from my right. I was the first Christian in my family. I knew only a handful of real-life Christians and even less about church.

At the time, I was pursuing music as a career. When that dream shattered, I cried out to God for the first time. Shortly after, I was in a small forest beside the Pacific Ocean. It was late. I couldn't see my hand in front of my face. I was wrapped in darkness, and for the first time I heard God whisper. I had a thought that I knew was not my own.

It was foreign to me. "Even if the darkness overcomes you, I am with you." I now knew this much about God, but I didn't know much else.

I discovered God's name about a week later when my vocal instructor, April, gave me *The Purpose Driven Life*. In those pages I discovered Jesus, our Immanuel: God with us. Everything clicked. I am never alone in the darkness. Because even if my eyes fail me, Jesus is with me.

Shortly after these first encounters with Jesus, I moved to Vancouver to start a degree in graphic design. I was surrounded by new friends and peers in my program. But when it came to my faith, I was going at it alone. My life wasn't easily split into "before" and "after" in those days. Faith came with me into my mess, though. A few months later, I fumbled into a freshly minted church plant.

I was fortunate to learn right away that the church isn't a building. It was a small and peculiar group of people who met in a modest home in East Vancouver.

There was Leighton. He had weak ankles and loved to play soccer anyway. In our conversations, he often referred to someone named Bonhoeffer. There was Anna, who was ceaselessly welcoming and thoughtful. I still remember when she told me that she wanted a relationship with God that includes washing the dishes. I wanted that too. There was Mike. He had a thick Scottish accent. Every week he had a story about meeting a stranger in a local thrift shop and telling them about Jesus. That felt like a little much to me at the time, but I respected his passion. There was Kyle. He asked great questions like, "What would it look like for us to do what Jesus says here?" I didn't always know what faith meant in practice, but Kyle helped me imagine it. And he made me want to discover it.

My initial impressions of this new church weren't flattering though. *These are not my people. I would never naturally spend time with any of them,* I remember thinking. It was partially true. But over time I discovered a gift greater than friendships centered around shared interests and hobbies. This church first modeled the ways of Jesus to me and made a life of faith plausible because they made it palpable. They were patient with my failings and insecurities. They walked with me as I stumbled toward grace. And they helped me pick up the pieces when my first engagement ended. I fell in love with these peculiar people as we ate together, spent time together, learned together, prayed together, grieved together, and loved together.

Next to the gift of salvation, I am convinced God's greatest grace is his people, his bride, our family: the church.

I love how people are greeted by name in the New Testament letters, especially at the end of Romans: Phoebe, Prisca, Aquila, Epaenetus, Mary, Andronicus, Junia, Ampliatus, Urbanus, Stachys, Apelles, Aristobulus, Herodion, Narcissus, Tryphaena, Tryphosa, Persis, Rufus (and his mom), Asyncritus, Phlegon, Hermes, Patrobas, Hermas, Philologus, Julia, Nereus (and his sister), and Olympas. That's twenty-nine ordinary people memorialized in Scripture because they were the names and faces of the church in Rome for Paul.

The church is always a gift composed of names and faces.

Years later, I discovered Leighton's favorite author for myself. In his classic book *Life Together*, the German pastor and Nazi dissident Dietrich Bonhoeffer writes, "The physical presence of other Christians is a source of incomparable joy and strength to the believer."[1] He continues, "Let him who until now has had the privilege of living a common Christian life with other Christians praise God's grace from the bottom of his heart."[2] The withward rhythm is all about embracing this immense privilege of life together *with* other followers of Jesus as a source of joy, strength, and gratitude.

Physical Presence

Bonhoeffer wrote well before the invention of the Internet and social media. The concept of "attending" church online or maintaining and developing relationships through various technologies beyond letter writing or (more rarely in his day) a phone call was not on his radar.

I do not want to dismiss how helpful technology can be in cultivating a relationship. The New Testament is proof that the early church embraced technology (letter writing, in their day) as one way of maintaining a sense of connection and continual formation. Yet the apostle John wrote, "I have much to write to you, but I do not want to use paper and ink. Instead, I hope to visit you and talk with you face to face, so that our joy may be complete" (2 Jn 1:12). Technology helps. But face to face is better.

The physical presence of other Christians is crucial to our formation and well-being. Whatever we do online or through other technologies should never be a replacement for gathering together in person (so long as meeting together is possible).

The author of Hebrews was the first to make Bonhoeffer's point, writing, "Let us consider how we may spur one another on toward love and good deeds, not giving up meeting together, as some are in the habit of doing, but encouraging one another—and all the more as you see the Day approaching" (Heb 10:24-25). Since its inception, the church has been tempted to give up meeting together. But there are spiritual benefits to physical presence. As Wesley Hill notes:

> God never meant us to be purely spiritual creatures. That is why he uses material things like conversations, shared meals and trips, hugs, small kindnesses, and gifts between friends to enrich the new life he's given us. We may think this rather crude and unspiritual. God does not: he invented human relationships. He likes friendship. He invented it.[3]

Only when we are physically present with one another can we experience the taste of a meal, the joy of a hug, the sound of Scripture read aloud, a hand on a shoulder in prayer, or the unique sense of connection that comes through eye contact and conversation.

Interdependence

Part of the reason we need the physical presence of others is because God made us as interdependent creatures. We are made in the image of the triune God. We are social beings by design. Research psychologists have demonstrated that our identity is coconstructed in relationship with others. We can only flourish and know ourselves in relationships.

This flies in the face of the independence and individualism that is often bred in the Western world. But when it comes to growth in Christlikeness, we can't do it alone. Consider the ample number of "one another" instructions throughout the pages of the New Testament. Since these are imperatives, they're not optional. But we can't "one another" ourselves. These commands are inconvenient because they challenge us to press into our life together with others in Christ.

The apostle Paul called the church "the body of Christ" for good reason. You are a member of the body; the body is not whole without you, and you are not whole without the body. A body will not thrive unless its parts function together in harmony. Once again, we can't do it alone. Our interdependence is a gift of our creation.

Surrendering Idealism

When we physically gather as interdependent Christians, idealism can sneak in as a disruptive guest.

I've met too many people who are disenfranchised with the church because it didn't live up to their ideals. They wanted a New Testament church: passionate and sacrificial like what we see in Acts. Or at the very least, they thought church relationships should be a lot easier and without conflict because we're all committed to the ways of Jesus. I affirm the desires of these people. But then I ask them to tell me which one they want specifically: Corinth? Ephesus? Pergamum? Laodicea?

The churches of the New Testament were diverse. Each one was uniquely flawed due to the influence of the culture around them and the lingering effects of sin at work in them. And all of the commands like "forgive one another" or "bear with one another" or "be patient with one another" imply that people will do things that require forgiveness, burden us, and test our patience. It's impossible to fulfill these commands if we run for the door the moment a church fails to live up to our ideals.

Bonhoeffer understood this, warning, "He who loves his dream of community more than the Christian community itself becomes a destroyer of the latter, even though his personal intentions may be ever so honest and earnest and sacrificial."[4] This idealism can pervade spiritual friendships too. Hill poignantly says, "I sometimes fantasize more about friendship than about friends."[5] It's easy for us to fall in love with the idea of community or friendship but fail to love our actual community and friends.

We must surrender our idealism. But this doesn't mean we settle for bland realism. The church is a community of faith, hope, and love—neither perfect nor defeated but a beautiful work in progress. Any gathering of Christians is a journey from being a pseudo-community to a true community.[6] In order for any community to truly flourish, there must be conflict and disappointment that expose how we've glossed over or ignored who we truly are in our life together. Only once we lay down our ideals and expectations—or our preference to ignore the challenges of all the "one another" commands—do we discover what it means to gather together in Christ. The journey together begins where we are and not where we think we ought to be (and especially not where we think someone else should be).

Withward Practices

The withward rhythm embraces the fact that our journey toward Christlikeness requires community and prioritizes gathering in the physical presence of other followers of Jesus. As you think about withward practices, ask yourself: Is my participation in the local church mostly for my benefit or for the overall health of the body? How can my gifts contribute to the church? Who do I need to journey alongside toward Christ?

While there are many practices that can be associated with this rhythm, I will once again explore three: table, spiritual friendship, and spiritual gifts.

Table. If you wanted to track down Jesus in ancient Palestine, you would likely find him at someone's home eating a meal. He frequently "reclined" at the table as a guest of the social outcasts and religious elites alike. It's no small thing that God incarnate shared meals with people. Some of the most astonishing miracles performed by Jesus had to do with food and drink: turning water into wine and multiplying loaves. And as New Testament scholar N. T. Wright wrote, "When [Jesus] wanted to fully explain what his forthcoming death was all about, he didn't give them a theory. He didn't give them a set of scriptural texts. He gave them a meal."[7] Eating is not some superfluous and functional activity. It is a practice where the physical and spiritual intermingle.

It's little wonder that sharing a meal together became a core practice of the early church (see Acts 2:42). It has remained a practice of the church throughout history. Our own table practices are part of the withward rhythm because we must be physically present and embrace interdependence to share a meal together.

One such practice is the Eucharist, which is also called the Lord's Supper or Communion. It requires that we prioritize gathering for worship on Sundays.

I must admit that it took me some time to appreciate the centrality of Communion. I knew Jesus instituted it at the Last Supper. I knew that churches kept doing it. But it just seemed like a ritual involving stale bread or wafers and a miniscule amount of wine or grape juice. It was odd. Things changed for me at a Good Friday service though.

When we were invited to draw near to Christ's table, it was as if time stopped behaving in a normal way. I sensed that I was walking up to Calvary where Christ was crucified. As I took the bread and the wine—whatever was happening in that moment—I participated in the benefits of Christ's death. I was forgiven because he was crucified. Overwhelmed by the sorrow and goodness of the cross, I started to cry.

The bestselling poet and essayist Kathleen Norris recalls one of her first spiritual awakenings. At a Catholic wedding she'd been invited to, she was astonished when the priest began to clean up the dishes after serving Communion. She writes:

> But I found it remarkable—and still find it remarkable—that in that big, fancy church, after all of the dress-up and the formalities of the wedding mass, homage was being paid to the lowly truth that we human beings must wash the dishes after we eat and drink. The chalice, which had held the very blood of Christ, was no exception. And I found it enormously comforting to see the priest as a kind of daft housewife, overdressed for the kitchen, in bulky robes, puttering about the altar, washing up after having served so great a meal to so many people. . . . After the experience of a liturgy that had left me feeling disoriented, eating and drinking were something I could understand. That and the housework.[8]

Whether through the bread and wine or the officiant as a "daft housewife" cleaning dishes, Jesus reveals himself at the table as our Host. He graciously welcomes us as his guests. When we draw near with faith and accept the bread and the wine, we draw near to Christ himself and participate in his presence, whether we're aware of it or not (1 Cor 10:16-17). And we keep at it, because this is his perpetual invitation (Mk 14:22-25; Lk 22:18-20; 1 Cor 11:23-25).

Every time we celebrate the Eucharist, we gather at the table of undeserving friends. The Lord's Table sets the stage and standards for our life together: it is not possible apart from the sacrifice of Jesus and his gracious invitation to participate in his life rather than clinging to our own. The table reminds us again and again that if we share in his bread and wine, we share in his body and blood, his death and resurrection. And it calls us to inhabit and embody his forgiveness and reconciliation together.

There is something unnerving about this, if we're honest. It means that people who are not like us are welcome at Christ's table. When Jesus was on earth, the Pharisee and prostitute ate side by side (Lk 7:36-50). Jews and Gentiles ate together (Gal 2:11-14). People once divided, unable to share a meal, laid aside their separation. Ethnocentric and racist attitudes were gutted and overcome. Slaves and masters shared meals together. Social divisions lost their power. But this is only possible when people acknowledge that Jesus is their Lord and host. It can only happen when lives are reoriented around Jesus and his ways.

We need the Lord's Table far more than we realize.

Of course, we can't always control how frequently we'll gather at the table. Although my preference is to receive Communion weekly, a brief survey of church history shows that the regularity of this practice has varied. If you're already rooted in a church, I urge you to respect their existing table practices (whether monthly or weekly or some other pattern). The one thing we can control is the preparation of our hearts to engage meaningfully at the table. We can also prioritize our weekly participation at worship gatherings, whether or not the table is set as part of the service. Gathering in the physical presence of other followers in worship cannot be neglected.

When it comes to our own table practices, the second aspect to consider is how we gather with other followers of Jesus outside of Sundays.

Most churches have some form of weekly groups, whether Bible studies or community groups or missional communities. In many cases, these weekly gatherings take place in someone's home, and often a meal is involved. But eating together can become a matter of function—something we pass through in order to get to the more important tasks of studying Scripture, praying together, or serving within the community. If we allow our Eucharistic practices to shape these gatherings too, though, then eating together is what sets the stage for all the other moments. What could our table practices look like at these gatherings?

Gavin and Joanne host a community group for their church. Once a week, they welcome other followers of Jesus as well as a few people exploring faith to their home. And every week, the evening begins around a shared meal. Everyone brings something to the table—whether a component of the meal or just their presence. As they eat together, they check in about how everyone is doing. They encourage people to share honestly and remind everyone to be gracious as they're all bringing different experiences and feelings into the evening. The rest of the time together might be used for Bible study or to pray for one another. Once a month, they host a meal at a low-income housing society to build relationships.

The Eucharist has shaped their gatherings in a few ways. One is that their group always remains open; because there's always more room at Christ's table there is always more room at their table. Over the years this has meant that their group has had to multiply, and other leaders had to be raised up. But it's also meant that their group has always looked a little different than they'd naturally expect.

As a practice, the table doesn't have to be tied to the formal structures of your church.

My wife and I have kept a sabbath together since our wedding day. The way we have engaged this practice has changed over the years to accommodate our schedules and the emergence of our children. But as we learned more about the ways people practice the sabbath, we realized that we were missing an important element: community.

Historically, the Sabbath was (and remains for Jewish people) a very relational day. You rested within a community. Comparatively, our own sabbath practice felt a little too small: it was us and our daughters. Julia and I decided to invite two other families to keep a weekly Friday evening sabbath meal with us. This became our sabbath kickoff. It's not exclusive; from time to time there are guests at the table. But usually it is composed of the same six adults and five children. Most Friday nights, we share a meal, we rotate who hosts, we rotate who cooks, we enjoy each other's company, and we ask the question, "Where did you see God at work this week?" The sabbath *with* others has become one of the lifegiving rhythms of my week.

When we host the dinner, we have a sabbath candle that the kids get to light to begin the meal. And when we light it we ask, "Why do we keep the sabbath?" The children answer, "Because God made the sabbath for us to rest," or something along those lines. But I've never forgotten the time my friend Christine responded. She said, "God made humanity on the sixth day, but their first real day of living was the sabbath. How beautiful is that?" Our sabbath dinner is a beautiful experience of living the way God intends. We were made to enjoy the gifts of God's presence, creation, and relationships with others. A simple meal helps us get a taste of it.

Our table practices can take many expressions. Whatever we may do, the table helps us prioritize physical presence and interdependence as we make room for others.

Brainstorm: What could table practices look like for you?

_____

_____

_____

Spiritual friendship. C. S. Lewis wrote, "Friendship is unnecessary, like philosophy, like art. . . . It has no survival value; rather it is one of those things which give value to survival."[9] In Western culture, romantic love is often celebrated as the most essential form of love for human flourishing. But the truth is that friendship gives value to life. The movement withward means adopting practices that help us invest in spiritual friendships.

Aelred of Rievaulx of the twelfth century wrote the short treatise *Spiritual Friendship*. He saw friendship as based on shared goals. This means there can be different kinds of friendship. For example, a friendship could be based on the shared pursuit of pleasure, such as going dancing or to a sports event. Or you could become friends with someone based on a mutual advantage or benefit, such as a business partnership. And then there's spiritual friendship, grounded in shared discipleship.

We should have a variety of friendships. But the withward rhythm emphasizes our need for spiritual friendships, because without them we will struggle to become the person God made us to be. As David Benner says, "My deepest and truest self is not an isolated self but finds itself only in the 'we' of community."[10] Spiritual friendships highlight our interdependence and the fact that we are made for relationships.

Spiritual friendship is sometimes associated solely with account-ability. And while accountability is an important dimension of any meaningful friendship, too often friendships that meet solely for that become performance measures rather than places where our brokenness can be met with grace and patience. Spiritual friendship involves a lot more than holding one another accountable. Wesley Hill describes it this way: "When I cannot feel God's love for me in my struggle, to have a friend grab my shoulder and say, 'I love you, and I'm in this with you for the long haul' is, in some ways, an in-carnation of God's love that I would otherwise have trouble resting in."[11] Such friendships require sacrifice, grit, long-suffering, and grace upon grace.

Shortly after I joined the little house church in East Vancouver, I was introduced to Jon. A mutual friend thought we would hit it off and encouraged us to spend some time together (thanks, Cato!). We did. And we've been inseparable since (except for the fact that we've never lived in the same city).

Jon and I have flown around the world together. I've made the nine-hour drive from Vancouver to Calgary to see him. He has made the same drive from Calgary to Vancouver to see me, supposedly in "seven hours." We've vacationed together. And since we've each married, our families have spent a little bit of time together here and there. But the primary way our friendship has flourished is through phone calls. Short and sometimes long but always frequent phone calls. While I was writing this book, my wife was shocked to learn that Jon and I speak on the phone roughly three-to-five times a week. She knew we talked a lot but not that much (Jon and I had a good laugh about the thought that we were possibly keeping it all a big secret). And we've been doing it for well over a decade.

Sometimes Jon and I talk about nonsense or about politics. But often we share what's going on in our lives. At times we have felt like we're running at the same pace toward Jesus together. But other times one of us is outpacing the other, and we encourage each other to catch up or slow down enough to help. But never do we feel like we're mismatched even if we're temporarily outpaced.

Our friendship is built on listening, offering perspectives, and pointing to Jesus. We laugh. We grieve. We pray, sometimes setting aside extra time on the phone to do just that. But usually we're just squeezing phone calls in between meetings. I live in downtown Vancouver, and if I have a five-to-fifteen minute walk somewhere, I call Jon.

It's doubtful that Jon and I will live in the same place before the new creation comes at Jesus' return. But his friendship is oxygen to my faith and soul. I have other friendships that have the same effect where it's easier to be physically present. I share this story about Jon, though, because it has taken years of intentionality to develop what we now have and enjoy. If you're just realizing you need better quality friendships, know that it will take time and effort to build them. But it's worth the investment.

Brainstorm: What could spiritual friendship look like for you?

_____

_____

_____

Spiritual gifts. Much like we need practices that keep us engaged in Scripture and rooted in prayer, we need practices that keep us living in our giftedness. While we cannot manipulate the Spirit in exercising our gifts—the Spirit can move through us as he sees fit in a given moment—in many cases he shows up when we are intentionally creating space to express our gifts. They are meant to be practiced.

For example, if you have the gift of teaching, how frequently will you exercise it? And don't assume that if you're not a pastor there won't be opportunities to teach. There are loads of environments for your gift to be practiced. Even time with just one friend can provide an opportunity to teach the Word and learn together. But another question is, what practices do you need to put in place to develop content and depth of knowledge so you have something worth saying?

I met with a recent seminary graduate who was working in construction. It's not his dream job, but it provides for his family. He had aspired to be a pastor. But a thorough discernment process helped him realize this was not his call. He is, rather, a remarkable teacher. His gift is undeniable. Because he works full-time, he commits to waking up two hours before his workday begins to study and write. He does this five days a week. This creates room for him to express his gift. He has since written and published a book. He told me, "I often feel God's pleasure when I write for his glory."

Or consider someone who has the gift of speaking in tongues; they too need to set aside time in their day to engage in this gift. Because even though it may sometimes be used spontaneously, Paul implies that it can also be used privately at our discretion when he calls it a gift for our personal edification (1 Cor 14:4). Presumably this means it can be a practice—perhaps part of our solitude with God. Or if you're like someone I know, maybe you'll replace listening to music on your morning drive with praying in tongues. Similarly, if you have the gift of intercession, you might make a practice of writing down prayer requests from people and setting aside time to pray.

My friend Gogo has the gift of encouragement. I have been on the receiving end of this gift many times, and I've noticed that he sometimes encourages spontaneously because it simply has become part of his personality, but he also does it in response to a prompting from the Holy Spirit. Discerning these promptings takes practice and a willingness to listen to the Spirit. Even so, the practice of encouraging others can be expressed through phone calls, letter writing, or meeting up over a coffee. You might even make a practice of setting aside an hour a week to pray and ask God who needs encouragement. Or encouraging could be part of your seasonal rhythm, instead of your weekly one.

When it comes to your rhythm for life, don't relegate your spiritual gifts solely to the realm of spontaneity. Intentionally put them into practice. Because your spiritual gifts are not just for your own benefit, but also for the common good of others.

Brainstorm: What could spiritual gifts look like in practice for you?

The Joy of People

The movie *Love Actually* begins with the now classic line, narrated in the Queen's English accent of Hugh Grant, "Whenever I get gloomy with the state of the world, I think about the arrivals gate at Heathrow Airport." I don't know about you, but if I'm feeling low, my go-to isn't visualizing an airport. The movie then serves up an emotional smorgasbord, however, as person after person greets each other with hugs and kisses and with love and joy shining in their eyes as they reunite with loved ones after time apart. Even those of us with robot-like emotions are strangely warmed.

The joy we feel toward those we love can be absolutely stunning, and it's amplified through time apart. As the saying goes, "Absence makes the heart grow fonder." The apostle Paul knew this. He wrote to the church in Philippi, "Therefore, my brothers and sisters, you whom I love and long for, my joy and crown, stand firm in the Lord in this way, dear friends!" (Phil 4:1). But Paul's love and joy were not only due to being physically distant from them. The unique connection we have with one another in Christ results in love and joy. When I take a big-picture view of how many names and faces have continued to fill out my vision of God's church, I'm filled with joy.

May the practices of your withward rhythm draw you into the flourishing that is only possible when we share our life together in Christ.

With: Examples

At the time of writing this book, this is my own withward rhythm.

Regular

- Weekly communion at St. Peter's
- Weekly sabbath dinner with friends
- Connect individually with Jon, Don, Alex, and Bub

- Weekly community group
- Preaching and teaching weekly (spiritual gift)
- One meeting per week to mentor/disciple a person

Seasonal

- Annual Canada Day long weekend with close spiritual friends
- Annual intensive with doctoral studies cohort

Growth

- Learn more about healthy sabbath practices with young children

This is Ruth's withward rhythm. She is in a committed relationship and works full-time as a counselor.

Regular

- Biweekly call with Mom
- Weekly Bible study
- Monthly meeting with other Christian counselors to pray for clients and share difficult cases
- Pray for use of gift of discernment and words of knowledge in sessions with clients (spiritual gift)
- Stick to eating plan to manage pre-diabetes

Seasonal

- Make financial donations at year end
- Quarterly meeting with spiritual director

Growth

- Learn more about cultivating spiritual friendship

WITH—COMMUNITY
Worksheet

Regular

_____
_____
_____
_____
_____
_____

Seasonal

_____
_____
_____
_____
_____
_____

Growth

_____
_____
_____
_____
_____

10

Out—Outward in Mission

As the Father has sent me, I am sending you.

JOHN 20:21

*Let love well up and stream through us as the
beat, pulse, and rhythm of our lives.*

JAMES H. OLTHUIS

ONE OF THE FEW TIMES I HAVE BEEN SPEECHLESS was when Julia
said to me, "I like you too." At the time we were newly acquainted
friends. On the day after Valentine's Day I bashfully said, "I like you."
I took the risk. I moved toward her. She reciprocated—and I was at
a loss for words.

When I first said "I love you" to Julia, however, she replied, "I *think*
I love you."

It worked out in the end.

When people move toward each other with love (or even "like"),
it's beautiful. And this experience is not limited to romantic love;
it's true with any gesture of love. Love *moves* toward another.

David Bosch, a renowned missiologist (a fancy title for someone
who studies the mission of God) in the twentieth century, once

wrote, "Since God is a missionary God, . . . God's people are a missionary people."[1] When the average person hears the word *missionary,* however, they think of people who travel overseas to proclaim the gospel to an unreached people group. Or perhaps they think of the person who goes overseas for a short-term mission trip to partner with a local group. Of course, this is part of what it means to be a missionary, but it's not the whole picture.

When I use the word *missionary* or even *mission,* I invite you to hear, "Love on the move."[2]

When Bosch declared that "God is a missionary God," he did not envision God fundraising, buying a plane ticket, and going off somewhere away from home to do mission. Nor was he suggesting that moving toward others with love is something God sometimes does. Rather, Bosch was reflecting on God's essential nature and character: God is love. And God moves toward his creation with love.

Think of how God sent his Son into the world for the sake of reconciling us to himself. God has a mission that flows out of his being. He is restoring all of creation—from galaxies to the fissures in the human soul—back into the harmony of his love. This is what makes him a missionary God.

We are made to reflect the movement of God's love toward the world, like children who grab their father's hands, place their feet on his feet, and attempt to walk in step with him. Yes, we're a little clumsy. We stumble a lot. But the strength of our Father keeps us balanced and moving in the right direction. Staying in step with his movement is a matter of holding on to the One who will not let us go.

As we join God's love on the move, we move outward. For some, this involves relocating to another state or province, or across the world. But for most of us it means staying where we are. And whether we're called to go or stay, we're invited to love our people and place out of the boundless reservoir of love available to us in the triune God.

Mission is nothing short of the call "to live and let love well up and stream through us as the beat, pulse, and rhythm of our lives."[3]

In doing so, we embody the advice of another acclaimed missiologist of the twentieth century, Lesslie Newbigin, who called the church to live in the kingdom of God in such a way that "people begin to ask the question to which the gospel is the answer."[4] Love captures the watching world's attention.

But let's not reduce mission down to evangelism. Evangelism is undeniably an indispensable part of our participation in God's mission. But there are innumerable ways we move outward that do not involve explicit evangelism, such as meeting the needs of the poor, foster parenting children, mentoring youth, or caring for creation. We just do those things with the wisdom of the apostle Peter in mind: "Always be prepared to give an answer to everyone who asks you to give the reason for the hope that you have. But do this with gentleness and respect" (1 Pet 3:15). This applies to all followers of Jesus, from the extrovert to the introvert, from the social butterfly to the quiet, shy, and reserved.

Evangelism aside, sometimes leaders such as myself create too much hype around mission and accidently foster a culture of guilt and obligation. I believe we should be excited about the mission of God. It is good news of great joy, after all (Lk 2:10). But we must be careful to continually trace any activity (such as evangelism, expressions of mercy, or pursuits of justice) back to its origin: love. That's the only way I know to relieve the pressure and burden that can arise around mission. God has moved toward us and all creation with love. We get to extend this movement toward others. It's that simple. Now *that* is something I want to be part of!

Depth for Breadth

The outward rhythm is about breadth. We move beyond ourselves and the relationships that nurture us toward our world with love. But we need depth for breadth. This rhythm can only spread wide if it runs deep. Through the other rhythms we cultivate a reservoir of spiritual health and vitality in order to generously share our lives and love with others. David Brooks calls this "the plunge inward and then the expansion outward."[5]

Tragically, we can neglect depth to focus on mission. The inner life can be seen as less important than the work of reaching others with the message of the gospel, showing mercy to those in need, or advocating for justice for the marginalized. We can give in to the tyranny of the urgent and all that needs to be accomplished and diminish the need to tend to a rich interior life.

But our spiritual reservoir will run dry if we lack depth. Jesus was clear: "Apart from me you can do nothing" (Jn 15:5). We must be with Jesus. Whatever we may accomplish to the neglect of our lives with Christ will be questionable at best, and of no eternal signifi-cance at worst. When we detach mission from abiding with Jesus, can we even call it mission? It can result in ministries crashing, per-sonal burnout, and even people walking away from faith.

Jesus invites us to hold depth and breadth together. He said, "As the Father has loved me, so have I have loved you. Now remain in my love" (Jn 15:9). To abide (or remain) in his love involves believing in him and continually being obedient to his ways of love. Because after his death and resurrection, he also said, "As the Father has sent me, I am sending you" (Jn 20:21). As we abide, we are sent. Jesus holds depth and breadth together in interdependence. If we have one without the other, we are malformed.

People

In being invited to join God's movement of love, we tend to want to stay in abstraction. It's one thing to quote the second greatest com-mandment, "Love your neighbor as yourself" (Lev 19:18; Mt 22:39), but to take it to heart, we have to fill in the picture of "neighbor" with vivid color.

Things change when you name your neighbor.

Love Grace who is rushed and tired as yourself.

Love Dave who works in finance and is eager to be your friend as yourself.

Love Charlie whose presence is a little intimidating as yourself.

Love Jamie and her bright extroversion as yourself.

Love Craig who is struggling through this season as yourself.

Love Diandra and her gaggle of children as yourself.

That requires more, doesn't it?

We are called to love people. Each has a name and story. We cannot love an amorphous sea of nameless faces.

And if we hold fast to the teaching of Jesus, "neighbor" even includes our enemies (Mt 5:44; Lk 10:25-37). Do we have the audacity to name the people we like the least and those we are inclined to hate? Do we have the courage to move toward them in love, even if it's expressed as a commitment to pray?

As you name the people God calls you to love, start by reflecting on your various roles. The outward rhythm is not exclusive to strangers and those who are yet to know Jesus. The first step outward is usually toward those we already know. It includes everyone God has entrusted to us to love. Yet we are to remain open to the people we do not know yet. The stranger, the orphan, the widow, the person in need, the person who is yet to believe in Jesus, and even the enemy are people with names and stories, worthy of love.

Place

As we seek to love our neighbor by knowing them, and as we try to expand the breadth of who we consider a neighbor, we always do so from a physical and real place.

In our global and digitally connected world, our sense of place can endlessly expand. But bigger isn't always better. As you think about place, don't be afraid of limits. Boundary markers can be a good thing. As Zack Eswine says, "What gives meaning to the world and glory to God is our love for him and for our neighbor in the place in which we have been called."[6]

When I was in a season of wrestling with my vocation as a pastor, I had the good fortune of meeting Kris, another pastor a few years ahead on the journey. He introduced me to the novels of Wendell Berry, suggesting I start with *Jayber Crow*. And he encouraged me to enjoy it by reading it slowly.

Although urban Vancouver is altogether different than the rural town of Port William in *Jayber Crow*, the book helped me realize that my calling is caught up with the people in the limits of my place. The mission of God takes place exactly where I am. It's not out there somewhere, over the hills, or relegated to some distant land. It does not require that I have global influence or be constantly engaged online. It's here. It is in the moments that make up my little life in the midst of an urban center.

Vancouver is my place. But I had to get more specific still. I started to look more closely at my neighborhood, the streets I walk every day, the stores I frequent—the small radius that makes up my daily life. The seawall, Emery Barnes Park, Farzad's Barbershop, Pallet Coffee, Nesters Market, and Robson Square. I, the Anglican priest, finally discovered my parish.

It's tempting to think that "mission" happens somewhere other than where we are. But there are boundless opportunities within the limits of our lives. That place matters.

Abraham Kuyper once said, "There is not a square inch in the whole domain of our human existence over which Christ, who is Sovereign over all, does not cry, 'Mine!'"[7] If you change diapers or cook meals, head to meetings or hire employees, care for friends or take time to build new relationships—none of these things are beyond the scope of God's mission. Love is on the move in the normal everyday realities that make up our lives. We can turn our attention to what is directly in front of us. We only need to be present to his presence in our place.

Outward Practices

Jesus calls us to breadth and depth. The outward rhythm is slanted toward our missional vocation. God's love is on the move among our people and place. We are called to point it out. Keep your spiritual gifts, talents, values, roles, and vocation in mind as you ask: How can I walk with Jesus as a witness to God's love on the move? Who am I called to love?

I want to consider three broad practices to spark ideas in your imagination: hospitality, generous service, and faith at work.

Hospitality. Ethicist Christine Pohl says:

> By definition, hospitality is gracious and generous. . . . Because Christian hospitality reflects divine hospitality. . . . In offering hospitality, practitioners live between the vision of God's kingdom in which there is enough, even abundance, and the hard realities of human life in which doors are closed and locked, and some needy people are turned away or left outside.[8]

The apostle Paul puts it simply: "Accept one another, then, just as Christ accepted you" (Rom 15:7).

This is the heart of hospitality.

For many of us, hospitality can start simply by reaching out to our neighbors. For example, Ryland was inspired by the book *The Art of Neighboring: Genuine Relationships Right Outside Your Door,* with questions like, "What good things might happen if you truly got to know the people in your neighborhood and they got to know you?"[9] He now is more intentional about getting to know his neighbors on his small street, going out of his way to introduce himself, have small or long conversations, and make himself available if anyone extends an invitation, shares a need, or expresses any interest in striking up a friendship. He eagerly welcomes people into his life and home because Christ has welcomed him.

If you're not sure how to practice hospitality, start by getting to know your literal neighbors. Let a relationship develop over time.

You don't need to rush it or find a way to squeeze a gospel presentation in right way. The Holy Spirit knows how to pace these things. But who knows what good things might happen if you start to love your actual neighbors?

The table is always a good place to start practicing hospitality and creating gracious space for relationships to develop and deepen. Vinay and his family host a monthly community meal at their small apartment. Although there are a few regulars and close friends, the understanding is that anybody is welcome to come. In fact, the expectation is that invitations will be regularly extended toward people who are lonely, isolated, or in need of friendship.

This simple practice is a way for Vinay to exercise his spiritual gift of hospitality for the good of the church and for those outside of it. The evenings only have a loose structure: set the table, eat a meal, invite people to share how their week has been, ask if there are any needs that can be prayed for, and then pray. The consistent practice, even on a monthly basis, allows meaningful relationships to develop over time. Inevitably, the topic of faith is a regular part of the conversation, because people want to understand why Vinay behaves the way he does. And to his surprise, many of his guests who are not yet followers of Jesus are eager to share their prayer requests.

Opportunities to practice hospitality may surprise you.

Manya has always had a passion for relational evangelism and building trust so that people can explore faith. When she retired she anticipated more time for these endeavors. But to her surprise, her church began to see an influx of new immigrants. Many of them needed help learning English.

Manya eagerly stepped into this opportunity.

She began creating hospitable environments in which to teach English, even providing tea and biscuits (in true *English* fashion). Although Manya can't immediately use her gift in evangelism, she takes pleasure in building relationships of trust and care as she helps people get their bearings in a new cultural environment. In some scenarios, Manya uses a children's Bible to teach English, and it leads to good conversation. More often, she is a conversation partner who listens to people's needs and offers to pray. Manya's outlook has changed. She now describes relational evangelism as hospitality evangelism: welcoming people, slowly and patiently, into the presence of God.

Practices of hospitality are built on the conviction that there can always be more room for new people in our lives, because there is always more room at God's table.

Brainstorm: What could hospitality look like for you?

Generous service. Jesus said, "The greatest among you will be your servant" (Mt 23:11) and, regarding himself, "The Son of Man did not come to be served, but to serve" (Mk 10:45). He also modeled this by getting on his hands and knees to wash his disciples' feet (Jn 13). The apostle Paul latched onto this as essential to Jesus' identity. In his "Christ hymn," the apostle declares that Jesus, as the Son of God, "made himself nothing by taking the very nature of a servant, being made in human likeness" (Phil 2:7). Since we reflect who Jesus is through our lives, it's no wonder Paul called the church to "serve one another humbly in love" (Gal 5:13). In serving, we walk in the ways of Jesus and demonstrate his nature. As we move with him, we join him on a downward descent into service.

Service is not beneath us. Nor is it to be done begrudgingly. Generous service is part of God's movement of love; we see this in the life of Jesus. So any practice of generous service can be an expression of God's mission and a critical part of the outward rhythm.

God invites us to be generous with ourselves along with our gifts, time, talent, and resources. Serving within our local church is essential. It takes many different members of the body contributing in varied ways for the whole body to flourish. When we serve our church, no matter what we're doing, it prepares us to go into our week willing to walk in the ways of Jesus. However, in the examples below I want to focus on what it can look like when we move outside the gatherings of our church to serve the neighborhood, city, or world around us.

Amelia works on rotation as a nurse. She loves her career. It is one way that she gets to live into her personal vocation "to help people discover holistic health." But outside of work, Amelia has taken on a new role as an entrepreneur. By hosting small seminars and workshops at community centers, schools, and churches in her neighborhood, she is using her gifts of teaching and leadership to educate people about physical, mental, and spiritual health and to help them create a road map to pursue holistic health. Amelia is convinced people can experience the "abundance" of life that Jesus offers in every domain of health. She has creatively connected her vocation, gifts, and values with generous service. Her story is a simple yet profound example of finding your unique place in God's mission.

Once a month, Rob joins a few people from his church to host a game night at a low-income housing society. They provide snacks and build relationships with residents over Scrabble, Jenga, and other fan favorites. Once in a while they go big and host a Bingo night. Over the years, these relationships have deepened and formed natural bridges to inviting people to get coffee or lunch, or even visit a Sunday service at his church. Together with his group, Rob generously serves those who are typically isolated, lonely, and without community. They provide connection, company, and friendship.

Although healthy relationships are usually reciprocal, sometimes we can express generous service by building a relationship with someone who may not be able to return the gift in the way we would expect. Over the years I have intentionally developed friendships with people who are sick, who have intellectual disabilities, or are in the darkness of a mental health issue. I am not suggesting that these people have nothing to offer in return; that is certainly not the case. What I am acknowledging is that sometimes it is an expression of generosity to share ourselves with others who may be limited in how much they can share themselves in return. I see this as an expression of service because grace is not about what someone gives in return but about what has been given to us.

Practices of generous service move us toward others with sacrificial love. As we meet the needs of others—whether physical, relational, or spiritual—we provide a glimpse of how Jesus has moved toward the world with generous service. The outward rhythm is by nature generous. We share what we have with others, whether it is our love, time, energy, gifts and talents, or resources.

Brainstorm: What could generous service look like for you?

Faith at work. It's important to briefly consider how we can express hospitality and generous service within the workplace, because the mission of God is not confined merely to the church and our spare time. For many of us, most of our days are spent at work. The average person will spend ninety thousand hours at work over their lifetime. This makes up roughly 40 percent of our time spent awake. We don't want to waste our lives. But more compellingly, Tim Keller says, "Our daily work can be a calling only if it is reconceived as God's assignment to serve others."[10] Finding creative ways to integrate our faith at work is essential to the outward rhythm.

Kristen is a high-school teacher who is committed to loving and caring for the holistic formation of her students. She prepares for her day by praying on her commute, asking God to empower her work and give her eyes to see her students as he sees them. She intentionally builds trust through listening well and attentively, and over the years she has built a reputation among students as someone they can talk to about their problems. And although she is not able to explicitly bring faith into the classroom environment at her school, she intentionally carves out time during her lunch period to pray for her students by name. If a student or coworker does initiate a conversation about philosophy, spirituality, or faith, Kristen will engage with gentleness and respect. The limitations on what she can or can't say related to her faith challenge her to trust that the Holy Spirit is able to answer her prayers and move in people's lives beyond her direct influence. She integrates her faith and work meaningfully by investing deeply in the formation of others through prayer.

Kevin works at a fast-paced tech start-up. The hours and demands are grueling. Quite often, employees are asked to give up evenings and weekends and sometimes even cancel vacations. The morale of Kevin's team fluctuates a lot. As upper management, he tries to integrate his faith at work by advocating for his team in various ways, including striving to humanize them among key decision-makers and arguing for his company to see employee well-being as part of the bottom line. His vision is slowly catching on, but it doesn't alleviate the pace.

Kevin also integrates his faith at work by refusing to give in to gossip and complaining. He knows his role has influence, and he seeks to reflect Christ's character through his own actions. He doesn't shut people down when they gripe, but he does invite them to consider proactive steps they can take to make changes. When he sees an employee struggling, he takes them out to lunch and listens. He also finds creative ways to care for his team using his spiritual gift of pastoring. When people ask him what he did on the weekend, he doesn't shy away from talking about his involvement at church. To his surprise, this often leads to interesting conversations and questions over time. And in some cases, he has invited coworkers to visit his church or try Alpha (a course to explore Christianity). Kevin's commitment to relational care and personal character is another way of engaging faith in work.

Of course, our efforts to integrate our faith into our work do not mean smooth sailing. It's not always easy. For several years I have provided pastoral care to Amber, who works in the animation industry. Like Kristen, she cultivates a hidden life of prayer. Like Kevin, she cares for her team and advocates for their well-being while tending to the quality of her own character. She knows she can shine as a light in her workplace. But the environment around her seems impermeable. She's seen no changes, and nothing looks like it is going to budge.

Even though she's been wounded by the abusive management and inhumane work hours, Amber has intentionally remained in this toxic work environment. She has considered leaving for another company, and it wouldn't be wrong if she did. But even in the bleakness, she is reminded, "Whatever you do, work at it with all your heart, as working for the Lord" (Col 3:23). She remains committed to integrating her faith at work by working for Jesus and not for results alone, no matter where she is.

Brainstorm: What could faith and work look like for you?

When Mission Finds You

While Julia and I lived in Orlando we lived in a duplex. A few months after we moved into it, a recently single mom and her toddler son moved into the unit connected to ours. I heard a knock on our door and opened it to meet Kelly for the first time. She seemed a little flustered and quickly got to the point: "Um, there's a snake in my apartment. Can you help me?"

I am from Victoria, BC, which is practically the opposite geographic and creaturely landscape of Orlando. It had taken me a long time to get my head around the concept of alligators in every body of water. I wasn't sure I was ready for snakes. But without thinking I blurted out, "Sure!"

I walked with her to her unit. All of her boxes were still outside in the heat. I opened the door to an empty space. The air conditioner had been off. It was hot. And there lay a twelve-foot (four-foot, according to Julia) black rat snake, happily curled up on the hardwood floor in the middle of the living room. I did not know if it was poisonous or not. But I had a broom and unwarranted confidence. I would sweep the snake out of the house.

After my first swipe, the snake coiled up and quickly went to strike me with a loud hiss. Thunder and lightning crashed in the background (it didn't). But over time I was victorious and swept the snake outside. It slithered quickly to the front yard and disappeared down into a little hole in the grass. Deeply bothered by its "nook," we all ran inside, locked the door, and started laughing.

If you didn't know this, now you do: snake-defeating heroes get invited over for dinner (just ask Jesus).

Once Kelly and her son were settled in, we had a lovely evening and dinner together. She was fascinated to learn that I was a graphic designer who had recently transitioned into a master's program in theology. When I told her about my studies in the Gospel of Mark, she couldn't get enough and asked question after question. She had never heard any of it before and was genuinely interested. Shortly after, she committed her life to the ways of Jesus.[11]

Amazing things happen when we embrace God's love on the move. But often the mission of God finds us. Especially if we are open to being interrupted from time to time, as Jesus was (see Mk 5:21-43, the story of Jesus with Jairus and the hemorrhaging woman, for an example).

I hope the different portraits I've shared in these practices help you see the multifaceted ways we can participate in God's mission. I've tried to highlight the ordinary ways people can engage in hospitality or generous service. Individually these stories might not seem like all that much. But when taken together, we can see how God uses each of us for his great work of redeeming and restoring this broken world.

If we pay attention to our people and place, we don't have to manufacture anything. As pastor Darrell Johnson says, "Evangelism is joining a conversation the Holy Spirit is already having with another person."[12] The practices we engage for the outward rhythm simply help us stay connected to what God is already doing in our midst.

May you always have an interruptible spirit prepared to join God's love on the move.

Out: Examples

This is Anna's outward rhythm. She is a stay-at-home mom.

Regular

- Invite families met at kids' preschool over for monthly play date

- Learn (and remember by writing down!) neighbors' names; learn birthdays and celebrate them intentionally

- Prioritize meal-trains in local church for people in need (sign up the day I see it!)

- Pray daily for the Holy Spirit to overflow in me with the joy of salvation

Seasonal

+ Kid-friendly service/volunteer opportunities in our city to engage with spouse and kids

Growth

+ Approach visits with extended family as opportunities to love deeply and share openly about my faith with parents and siblings

This is Emmanuel's outward rhythm. He is a young lawyer in an urban setting.

Regular

+ Serve on hospitality team at my church twice a month

+ Support church staff with simple pro-bono legal counsel as needed

+ Learn names of janitorial staff at my office; treat them with utmost respect (as I would the senior partners)

+ Frame Micah 6:8 at my desk as my values guide for legal practice; engage conversation with coworkers on faith if they ask

Seasonal

+ Invite neighbors in our hall (even the one who drives me crazy) over for dinner quarterly

+ Attend conference of Christian lawyers on advocating for kingdom values through law

Growth

+ Stretch myself in Scripture memorization with my wife; ask God to give us opportunities to share his Word

OUT—MISSION
Worksheet

Regular

Seasonal

Growth

Epilogue

Godspeed

Jesus went on from there and walked beside the Sea of Galilee.
And he went up on the mountain and sat down there.

MATTHEW 15:29 (ESV)

If you could do it, I suppose, it would be a good idea to live
your life in a straight line.... But that is not the way I have done it, so far.
I am a pilgrim, but my pilgrimage has been wandering and unmarked.
Often what has looked like a straight line to me has been a
circling or a doubling back.... And yet for a long time,
looking back, I have been unable to shake off
the feeling that I have been led.

WENDELL BERRY

CHIMES ARE RINGING. They start quietly but slowly grow in volume. Julia wakes up and turns the alarm off on her phone. It's 6:30 a.m. She thinks, *Do I really want to get up this early?* As she sits up, her husband (aka me) is quick to reclaim a new allotment of bed space. The kids are still asleep and the floor is cold, but at least the house is quiet for now.

She makes a cup of tea, curls up in her favorite chair, opens her Daily Offices, and prays the invitation, "If you remain in me and I in you, you will bear much fruit; apart from me you can do nothing." She sits in silence, not fully awake yet. But she tries to be present to the presence of Jesus. "Immanuel ... you are with me," she says. Then she prays the age-old words, "Our Father in heaven ..." But when she gets to the end of the Lord's Prayer, she realizes that her attention has drifted off. She prays it again. And this time she is a little more present to it.

Julia reads her daily passages of Scripture and then opens her journal. But before she can write a word or reflect much at all, she hears the pitter-patter of two sets of energetic feet rushing down the stairs. She looks at the clock. It's 6:50. The girls are up earlier than they should be.

Taking another sip of her tea, Julia looks up at the faces of her daughters and says, "Good morning, my loves." She knows she can pray later in the day. But the day ends up being full. She has moments of gratitude and exasperation, both expressed in quick prayers: "Thank you, Jesus." "Help me, Jesus!" At least there will be time to focus in prayer when the kids are asleep. After a demanding day, however, Julia climbs into bed to pray the Daily Offices and falls asleep.

Then chimes start to ring.

Our rhythms don't always go as planned. Sometimes our practices are interrupted. Because life isn't always tidy and tamed. This brings us back to the question, "Why would we have a rhythm for life?"

An interrupted rhythm is better than no rhythm at all. The point of a rhythm isn't rigidity but elasticity. We need a rhythm because spontaneity and strict planning both carry risks. If you don't know where you're going, you may never arrive. Or you may end up right back where you started. And even if you do know where you're going, you may get there but miss that God wanted you somewhere else.

We don't want to exchange dependence on the Holy Spirit for a rhythm for life. Neither do we want to mistake "winging it" for the work of the Spirit. Life with the Spirit is often somewhere between spontaneity and planning—and sometimes way out in left field, or second base, or outside the stadium altogether. Perhaps the Spirit isn't even into sports metaphors.

Your Rhythm for Life

If the path to Christlikeness was a perfectly straight line, this book would be an exercise in drawing that line with your wrong hand and without a ruler.[1] We do not control the Holy Spirit. As Jesus says, "The wind blows wherever it pleases. You hear its sound, but you cannot tell where it comes from or where it is going" (Jn 3:8). If we could determine every step of our walk with God, it would no longer be a relationship. And after some time, it would likely get boring.

You can't tame the living Spirit of God. You can only live in pursuit of one another. Your rhythm keeps you in the pursuit.

The first part of this book helped you discern who God has made you to be. This was the blueprint for the second part—discovering rhythms for living into your vocation. It's time to bring the two together. Does the house match the blueprints? Will the practices you identified help you become who God has made you to be?

Start in pencil.

Write down your personal vocation statement. And take a moment to consolidate the practices you identified for up, in, with, and out.

RHYTHM FOR LIFE

Personal vocation statement:

_____

_____

_____

_____

Regular

Up: _____

_____

_____

_____

In: _____

_____

_____

_____

With: _____

_____

_____

_____

Out: _____

_____

_____

_____

Seasonal

Up:

_____

_____

_____

_____

In:

_____

_____

_____

_____

With:

_____

_____

_____

_____

Out:

_____

_____

_____

_____

Growth

_____

_____

_____

_____

_____

As you see all the practices together, how do you feel?

If you happen to feel overwhelmed, remember: your rhythm for life shouldn't complicate your life or make it busier. Don't bombard yourself with spiritual practices. Often, the first draft of a rhythm is blatantly unrealistic and naively optimistic. If your rhythm looks burdensome, reconsider what you have on it. The goal is to focus on the essential practices that respect your current season of life and help you become the person God has made you to be. And really, the more we remove, the more we can focus on what matters. Simplify. If you can't memorize most of your rhythm for life, it is too complex. Stick to the essentials. If you had nothing to prove, what would you remove? What can be erased? What is necessary to keep the path toward Christlikeness in focus? Pay attention to the practices that keep you rooted in Christ and a sense of his closeness.

If a rhythm for life is new for you, you might reduce your practices down to one for each rhythm. You could even focus on one rhythm at a time, working, for example, on your upward practices for a month or several months and then exploring your inward rhythms once you feel settled in the upward ones, and so on. And if your rhythm for life doesn't move you toward dependence on the Spirit and growth in Christlikeness, throw it out and start a new one. Even if your rhythm is working for you, you will want to consider new practices and expressions from time to time.

Once you have a rhythm for your current season, find creative ways to keep it at the forefront of your mind until it becomes second nature. You might want to create a version and place it where you'll see it regularly: beside your bed, inside your Bible, on your fridge, on your phone background, or at your workspace, for example. The most helpful way to stay on track is to check in once a month, quarterly, or annually with close spiritual friends—and then revise your rhythms together.

Godspeed

With your rhythm for life in hand, you're ready to embark on the journey toward Christlikeness with more intentionality. But first, consider the tempo.

The short film *Godspeed* chronicles the journey of Matt Canlis, an American pastor whose desire to change the world came to a halt in a Scottish parish.[2] Canlis reflects on the pace of our lives as Christians and asks, "What is the pace of Jesus?"

In our cultural moment, we are in such a rush. We want to get where we're going quickly. It's hard for us to conceive of "a long obedience in the same direction."[3] But this is the essence of the Christian pilgrimage.

Could it be that God is not as hurried as you are?

Think about how "Jesus went on from there and walked beside the Sea of Galilee. And he went up on the mountain and sat down there" (Mt 15:29 ESV). We can overlook the very human details of the gospel. Jesus walked from place to place. He did so at approximately three miles an hour. This is literally God's speed on earth.

We don't need to outpace Jesus.

Godspeed invites us to slow down and be present—with Jesus, with ourselves, with others, and with our world. N. T. Wright puts it this way: "We're slowing down to catch up with God."[4] As you move in the four rhythms—upward to God, inward to self, withward in community, and outward in mission—the tempo is Godspeed. It is the only pace that respects how God meets humanity in our mess and beauty.[5]

You Will Arrive

Godspeed is typically used as a way to wish success or God's favor upon someone as they set off on a journey. And I want to use it in this sense as well. As you journey toward Christ—Godspeed!

Rhythms for life bring intentionality into our pursuit of Jesus. But we do not need to anxiously rush toward our destination, stressed about all that needs to be done and all that needs to improve. We can't expect ourselves or anyone else to get it all right, all the time, right away. That's not the goal. As Ken Shigematsu writes, "The goal of having a rule is not to achieve a 'balanced life' per se, but to live with Christ at the center of all we do."[6] Nothing more and nothing less.

If Jesus is at the center of all you do, then you have the freedom to move at the pace he sets rather than be driven by anxiety, the need to perform, or anything else. Because you will arrive at Christlikeness. As the apostle Paul wrote, "[Be] confident of this, that he who began a good work in you will carry it on to completion until the day of Christ Jesus" (Phil 1:6). As you continue on this journey, you can walk with the assurance that your destination is just around the bend—and Jesus will bring you all the way home.

Godspeed.

Gratitudes

THIS BOOK STARTED OUT AS A SMALL IDEA that took on a life of its own. Many people were involved in midwifing it. I am indebted to Marley Campbell and Preston Gordon. Your ideas and influence are like fingerprints all over this book. It would not exist without you, and it was a joy to write with you. I want to thank the many people of St. Peter's Fireside who gave their input, worked through numerous iterations, and engaged in our rhythms for life retreats. Their patience and thoughtfulness vastly improved the final work. This book is truly a product of the church for the church.

I am grateful to Brandon O'Brien at Redeemer City to City as well. A happy outcome of this project is how it turned us into friends. Thank you for making me feel like a real writer and for your part in bringing this book to a wider audience. This book was also made possible by a generous grant from the Forum for Theological Exploration. Thank you to Roger Revell for securing this grant, but also for being Roger Revell.

In addition, I want to thank Al Hsu, Andrew Bronson, and everyone at InterVarsity Press. I am humbled that you want to help others connect with what I've written.

Most of all, I want to thank Julia, Ansley, and Magnolia—you are the harmony to the melody of Jesus in our rhythms. I see God's love on the move in each of you—and I'm grateful to be yours.

And thank you.

Although we may never meet, I am grateful for your time and effort to journey into rhythms for life.

Crafting Your Rhythms for Life in Community

Once you've identified who you will work through this book with, you should set clear and simple expectations for each meeting. As a baseline, I suggest that each person will have read the assigned chapter and prayerfully engaged in the worksheets. To help instill this standard, you can randomly select who will summarize the chapter by spinning a pencil (thanks to Mark Sayers for this quirky practice in *Reappearing Church*). I would also encourage everyone to turn off their cell phones during your time together.

As you work through this book, it's better to go slow and be consistent, because discerning our vocation and integrating new practices take time and should not be rushed. If you follow the schedule below it will take 16 weeks.

Group Schedule: 1 Hour

- **Five minutes:** Read the opening quotes from the beginning of the chapter. Start your time in thanksgiving and praise. Pray together for God's guidance.

- **Ten minutes:** Spin the pencil/pen to see who will share a summary of the chapter, and then listen (or share).

- **Twenty-five minutes:** Talk through the chapter.

   ◊ *For part one:* Discuss the worksheets (or work through them together): Where did you find clarity? Where are you struggling? Where might you need to dwell a little longer? What were your aha moments?

   ◊ *For part two:* Dedicate two weeks for each chapter (chapters seven through ten). For the first week, discuss the content and create a plan to experiment with practices. For the second week, share about the practices you tried and how you encountered God through them.

- **Five minutes:** Ask each other how you'll integrate what you're learning into your rhythm for life.

- **Fifteen minutes:** Pray for one another to be deeply formed into the image of Christ through this process.

If you would like a free workbook and supporting videos to help you engage *Rhythms for Life* in greater depth, please visit www.alastairsterne.com/rhythms/together.

Resources for Spiritual Practices

THERE ARE A PLETHORA OF BOOKS on spiritual practices. I have only explored a handful of practices: solitude with God, gratitude, sabbath, self-examination, stewardship, guidance, table, spiritual friendship, spiritual gifts, hospitality, generous service, and faith and work. And I've barely scratched the surface of each of these, let alone the breadth of other options. Below are a few recommendations of resources that will allow you to explore some of these practices in more depth or increase your awareness of other options.

Start Here

Adele Ahlberg Calhoun, *Spiritual Disciplines Handbook*

Dorothy Bass, *Practicing Our Faith: A Way of Life for a Searching People*

David Fitch, *Seven Practices for the Church on Mission*

Richard Foster, *Celebration of Discipline*

Go Deeper

Randy Alcorn, *Money, Possessions, Eternity*

Dan Allender, *Sabbath: The Ancient Practices*

Ruth Haley Barton, *Invitation to Solitude: Experiencing God's Transforming Presence*

John Mark Comer, *The Ruthless Elimination of Hurry*

Michael Casey, *Sacred Reading: The Ancient Art of Lectio Divina*

Ian Cron and Suzanne Stabile, *The Road Back to You: An Enneagram Journey to Self-Discovery*

Robert Emmons, *Thanks! How Practicing Gratitude Can Make You Happier*

Wesley Hill, *Spiritual Friendship*
Timothy Keller, *Every Good Endeavor: Connecting Your Work to God's Work*
Christine Pohl, *Living into Community: Cultivating Practices That Sustain Us*
Sam Storms, *The Beginner's Guide to Spiritual Gifts*

A Simple Guide to Discerning a Call to Ministry

IT WAS AN ORDINARY, WARM, SUNDAY NIGHT IN ORLANDO. I attended the evening service at my church and then went out for dinner with a few friends. We took a table on the patio. Our conversation circled around many topics. Eventually it landed on ministry. At that point in time I was feeling inexplicably drawn toward ministry. I shared a little about that, and then my friend Andy, a seasoned worship pastor, piped up, saying, "If you can do anything else, do it. But I have a feeling you can't."

The words carried a weight I could feel. But I also hoped he was right—which felt odd.

I've since heard many other seasoned ministers repeat this advice in their own words. I've said similar things too.

But as I discerned my own call to ministry, I thought Andy and Spurgeon were a little extreme. I had other paths before me. I enjoyed my previous career in design. But I see the wisdom of their words now. Because the call to ministry is not for the faint of heart.

If you are called to ministry, it is not merely one of many options; it is something you must do. The sense of your call compels you to it, even though you might have other talents. But how do you discern if you really are called? Let me offer a few simple guidelines.

First, I want to demystify the "call" to ministry a little bit. If your ministry is pastoral care or preaching or evangelism or leading in some formal capacity within a church, there is an element of a "call." But *pastor* is first and foremost a role. Yes, it's one that requires unique discernment. But it is helpful to remember that our call (or vocation) is to follow Christ into Christlikeness. The question around ministry is actually, "Is Jesus leading me into a specific role in ministry, such as a pastor?"

Second, in discerning whether Jesus is leading you into ministry, focus on character. Become overfamiliar with the qualifications for deacons and elders in 1 Timothy 3:1-7 and Titus 1:6-9, because your deepest vocation is always Christlikeness. You need character to step into ministry, character to sustain ministry, and character to last after ministry. While no one in ministry is without fault, you need to be qualified in character.

Third, do not try to discern this alone. You must involve your community of faith. Each denomination has its own discernment process. Reach out to your leaders and ask them what the process entails and how you can begin. And then, so long as it is a community you trust, submit to the process. Engage prayerfully and carve out time to be with God.

Fourth, pay attention to your inward sense of calling and the outward affirmation of calling. Both are necessary—and both are present when someone is called by God into the work of ministry. Whether you have a slow-growing desire for ministry that you can't shake off, an odd attraction to ministry, a dramatic spiritual encounter, or some other sense that you can't explain, there must be a personal sense of calling. Others encouraging you to go into ministry or saying you would be suited for the work is not enough if you don't have a personal, inward call to ministry.

You also need outward affirmation of your call. There must be people around who benefit from your love and service, and who can affirm that you are well-suited for the work. It is not enough to feel personally called when many people who know you say you should not go into ministry.

Tim Keller offers a helpful approach to navigate the inward and outward balance, identifying three elements to a call: ability, affinity, and opportunity.[1] Do you have the ability—the skills and spiritual gifts required? Do you have the affinity—a desire and burden to meet human need and the spiritual maturity to do so? Do you have opportunity—do the proverbial doors open up and do others benefit or affirm your service? If so, you may be called.

Fifth, do not use the urgency of the gospel to justify hurrying into ministry. This is hard to do, but discerning a call into ministry always requires patience. Too often I have met people who are in a rush because the gospel is of such importance. This is true. But you do not need to be ordained or recognized as a pastor in order to give your life to serving others and proclaiming the gospel. And a healthy approach to the process rarely moves along quickly, because maturity and character are required. Discernment takes time. So embrace patience.

Finally, I am convinced that if you craft a healthy rhythm for life, discernment will be much easier. Embrace the spiritual practices that help you become who God calls you to be. As you do, you'll have the habits and disciplines to serve you both in discernment and in ministry.

May you always go where Jesus calls you to go.

Notes

Introduction: Rhythms for the Journey

[1] Frederick Buechner, *The Sacred Journey: A Memoir of Early Days* (San Francisco: HarperCollins, 1982), 6.

[2] Maisie Ward, *Return to Chesterton* (New York: Sheed and Ward, 1952), 137.

[3] If you would like to explore this further, I recommend *Union with Christ* by Rankin Wilbourne. It's the kind of book that inspires you to put it down to talk to Jesus.

[4] Dallas Willard, "Live Life to the Full," Renovaré, accessed March 26, 2019, https://renovare.org/articles/live-life-to-the-full.

[5] Benedict of Nursia, *The Rule of St. Benedict* (London: SPCK, 1931), 2.

[6] *Book of Common Prayer*, General Synod of the Anglican Church of Canada (Toronto: Prayer Book Society of Canada, 1962).

1 Identity

[1] If you have experienced any form of abuse, I highly encourage you to find a qualified Christian psychologist or counselor in your area (I do not recommend "biblical counseling"). If you've experienced any form of sexual abuse as a child, I recommend *The Wounded Heart* by Dan Allender. It can take a long time to disentangle from contamination stories. There is nothing wrong with you if you're not healing at the speed you'd like. Skip ahead and read the epilogue, "Godspeed," before going any farther.

[2] When I use the word *story* in this way, I am not implying that the story of God is fictitious. It's not. And in a sense it's more real than it is nonfiction: it is the true living story of the world. I use the phrase "story of God" in a broad sense to describe the grand and overarching narrative of Scripture: creation, fall, redemption, new creation. To learn more about this, read *The Drama of Scripture* by Craig G. Bartholomew and Michael W. Goheen.

[3] If you want a deeper historical reflection on the nature of the Trinity, read the Athanasian Creed.

[4] Queen, "Somebody to Love," *A Day at the Races*, Elektra Records, 1976.

[5] Stanley M. Hauerwas, *The Peaceable Kingdom: A Primer to Christian Ethics* (Notre Dame, IN: University of Notre Dame Press, 2011), 31.

[6] I realize all this talk of creation, Adam, Eve, and sin stirs a lot of questions. If you want to learn more, I recommend *Confronting Old Testament Controversies* by Tremper Longman III.

[7]This quote is from one of William Barclay's Daily Study Bible commentaries. I wish I could tell you which one. Instead, I would encourage you to read any of them so long as you keep in mind that Barclay's metaphysical world is a little too small at times.

[8]John Calvin, *Commentaries of The First Book of Moses called Genesis* Volumes I & II (Woodstock, NY: Devoted Publishing, 2018), 32.

[9]Each of the Synoptic Gospels records three instances of Jesus revealing to his disciples why he came into the world: Mt 16:21-23; 17:22-23; 20:17-19; Mk 8:31-33; 9:30-32; 10:32-34; and Lk 9:21-22; 9:43-45; 18:31-34.

[10]Timothy Keller, *The Meaning of Marriage: Facing the Complexities of Commitment with the Wisdom of God* (London: Hodder & Stoughton, 2013), 43.

[11]J. I. Packer, *Knowing God* (Downers Grove, IL: InterVarsity Press, 1993), 207.

[12]James Finley, *Merton's Palace of Nowhere* (Notre Dame, IN: Ave Maria Press, 2018), 30.

2 Gifts, Talents, and Personality

[1]If you would like a brief summary of each spiritual gift take a look at spiritual giftstest.com/spiritual-gifts. There are also great books such as *The Beginner's Guide to Spiritual Gifts* by Sam Storms.

[2]John Piper, "What Is Speaking in Tongues?," Desiring God, January 30, 2013, https://www.youtube.com/watch?v=jzipsG3-S6A.

[3]Jon Thompson said this but I know not where. I do know that Jon Thompson has the spiritual gift of explaining the spiritual gifts.

[4]Today there are many popular personality tests, such as Myers-Briggs, the Enneagram, and StrengthsFinder. As useful tools for self-reflection, such tests can help you articulate your own inclinations, desires, and emotional reactions, and see your weaknesses, shortcomings, and blind spots. They should never be given the power to define who you are, though, and must be balanced by a scriptural vision of the whole person.

[5]If you're intrigued by this thought I recommend reading *Prayer and Temperament* by Chester Michael and Marie Norrisey.

[6]If you want to help your church create a conversation around mental health, I commend the Sanctuary Course to you (sanctuarymentalhealth.org).

3 Virtuous Values

[1]The origin of how we use the word *values* today is traced to Friedrich Nietzsche (Gertrude Himmelfarb, *The De-moralization of Society* [New York: A. A. Knopf, 1994], 10). Having declared that "God is dead," Nietzsche proposed that humanity must move past archaic notions of revelatory and objective standards of good and evil or virtue and vice. Rather, he called people to create values. Ever since, values

have become a subjective way of determining morality and matters of importance. Since the language of values is no longer exclusive to the realm of economics and is part of the cultural air we breathe, I choose to use the term—albeit carefully.

[2]I am indebted to Dave Phillips for this delightful phrase. I found it in his self-published book *Three Big Questions That Everyone Asks Sooner or Later* (2006).

[3]Richard Barrett, *The Values-Driven Organization: Unleashing Human Potential for Performance and Profit* (Abingdon, UK: Routledge, 2014), 3.

[4]According to my notebook, Tomas Eneroth said this. According to Google, it was Maureen Metcalf. God only knows.

[5]Brian P. Hall, *Values Shift: A Guide to Personal and Organizational Transformation* (Eugene, OR: Wipf & Stock, 2006), 24.

[6]Jerry Seinfeld, "Jerry Seinfeld on Halloween (Stand-up in New York)," October 31, 2009, https://www.youtube.com/watch?v=MarBVyZVe9s.

[7]Sam Storms, *Hope of Glory—100 Daily Meditations on Colossians* (Downers Grove, IL: InterVarsity Press, 2008), 35.

[8]Catechism of the Catholic Church (Vatican City: Libreria Editrice Vaticana, 1994), article 7.

[9]Harper is not her real name. But if you're looking for a good name for a baby, I commend it to you.

[10]Hall, *Values Shift*, chapter 2.

4 Roles

[1]Shakespeare, *As You Like It*, 2.7.

[2]I want to clarify that I am standing on the orthodox ground of economic, relational, or functional subordination in the Trinity contrary to the heterodox position of ontological subordination. If none of these terms mean anything to you, don't worry about it. This footnote is for the theologically sensitive.

[3]I suggest you read the Psalter and highlight anytime you see a role used as a metaphor for God. You'll be surprised by how often it occurs and how varied the roles are.

[4]I picked up this specific quote from a Tim Keller tweet/truth bomb. I suspect it is from *Counterfeit Gods*, which you should go ahead and read if you haven't.

[5]If you self-harm or have thoughts of suicide, please reach out to someone or a hotline. You do not need to be ashamed. You do not have to face your pain alone. There are trustworthy people who can journey with you.

5 Vocation

[1]Simon Sinek, *Start with Why: How Great Leaders Inspire Everyone to Take Action* (London: Penguin Business, 2019), 39.

[2]Steven Garber, *Visions of Vocation: Common Grace for the Common Good* (Downers Grove, IL: InterVarsity Press, 2014), 18.

[3]I first heard this phrase from Dr. Brian D. Russell in a class at Asbury Theological Seminary.

[4]This phrase originates from theologian and missionary Lesslie Newbigin.

[5]Henri J. M. Nouwen, *Beyond the Mirror* (New York: Crossroad, 1990), 12.

[6]Frederick Buechner, *Wishful Thinking: A Seeker's ABC* (London: Mowbray, 1994), 118.

[7]James Martin, *Between Heaven and Mirth: Why Joy, Humor, and Laughter Are at the Heart of the Spiritual Life* (New York: HarperOne, 2012), 121.

[8]Buechner, *Wishful Thinking,* 119.

[9]Yes, you read that correctly. Bub is his name, or as he often says, "Bub not Bob, just B-U-B."

[10]David Brooks, *The Second Mountain: How People Move from the Prison of Self to the Joy of Commitment* (New York: Random House, 2019), 111.

[11]I know this point is contested.

[12]Malcolm Guite, "Interview Series with Malcolm Guite—Part 1," interview by Lancia E. Smith, Cultivating, September 30, 2019, https://thecultivatingproject .com/interview-series-with-malcolm-guite-part-1/.

[13]Brooks, *The Second Mountain,* 93.

[14]Scott Cormode, "Vocation and Leadership," June 9, 2017, produced by FULLER Studio, 2:41, https://www.youtube.com/watch?v=NiCr2epOoN8.

[15]Martin, *Between Heaven and Mirth,* 134.

[16]If you've struggled to discern your personal vocation, do not stress. Instead, breathe and remember that it can take time. You may need to schedule a retreat, find a place for solitude, meet with a spiritual director, or talk with trusted friends, family, and mentors.

6 Crafting a Rhythm for Life

[1]"Elite Athletes Spend 10,000 Hours Training for London 2012," Inside the Games, November 18, 2010, https://www.insidethegames.biz/articles/11108/elite-athletes -spend-10000-hours-training-for-london-2012.

[2]James K. A. Smith, *You Are What You Love: The Spiritual Power of Habit* (Grand Rapids, MI: Brazos, 2016), 25.

[3]The up, in, out language is hardly an original paradigm. When I first began to use this language in my own ministry, I drew richly from the pastor and consultant Michael Breen. The "with" language I coopted from Mars Hill Bible Church in Grand Rapids, Michigan.

[4]If you would like to learn more about this dimension of practices, consider reading *The Dangers of Christian Practice* by Lauren Winner.

[5]Charles Spurgeon, "Peace by Believing," The Spurgeon Center, accessed March 11, 2020, https://www.spurgeon.org/resource-library/sermons/peace-by-believing/.

7 Up—Upward to God

[1]I personally use a more accessible version of the Daily Offices that my church releases each year. You can download a copy at stpf.ca/prayer. If you prefer an app, try Daily Prayer at rethinkme.com.

[2]Robert A. Emmons, *Thanks! How Practicing Gratitude Can Make You Happier* (New York: Houghton Mifflin, 2008), 2.

[3]Emmons, *Thanks!*, 9, 55.

[4]I am a sucker for aesthetics. If you are too, you'll enjoy *5 Year Diary* designed by Tamara Shopsin.

[5]Rick Hanson, *Hardwiring Happiness* (New York: Harmony Books, 2015).

[6]Ross A. Lockhart, *Lessons from Laodicea: Missional Leadership in a Culture of Affluence* (Eugene, OR: Cascade Books, 2016), 106.

[7]Peter Scazzero, *The Emotionally Healthy Leader: How Transforming Your Inner Life Will Deeply Transform Your Church, Team, and the World* (Grand Rapids, MI: Zondervan, 2015), 144.

[8]Jacqueline Lapsley, "A Happy Blend: Isaiah's Vision of Happiness (and Beyond)," in *The Bible and the Pursuit of Happiness: What the Old and New Testaments Teach Us About the Good Life*, ed. Brent A. Strawn (New York: Oxford University Press, 2012), 83.

[9]Annie Dillard, *The Writing Life* (New York: Harper Perennial, 2013), 23.

8 In—Inward to Self

[1]There is much folklore around this story. If you want to learn more see winstonchurchill.org/publications/finest-hour/finest-hour-148/the-1954-sutherland-portrait/.

[2]Saint Augustine, *Confessions* (Oxford: Oxford University Press, 2008), Book X.

[3]Saint Basil, *The Hexaemeron* (Edinburgh: Aeterna, 2016), Homily X.

[4]John Calvin, *Institutes of the Christian Religion*, ed. John T. McNeill, trans. Ford Lewis Battles, Library of Christian Classics, vol. 20 (Philadelphia: Westminster, 1960), 1.1.1 and 1.1.2.

[5]Klyne Snodgrass, *Who God Says You Are: A Christian Understanding of Identity* (Grand Rapids, MI: Eerdmans, 2018), chapter 1.

[6]The law of Thelema is not explicitly in the mouth of Satan in Scripture. However, it expresses Satan's desire for us to rebel against God. "Do what thou shalt wilt" was founded and popularized in the twentieth century by the occultist Aleister Crowley.

[7]David G. Benner, *The Gift of Being Yourself: The Sacred Call to Self-Discovery* (Downers Grove, IL: InterVarsity Press, 2015), 54, emphasis mine.

[8]Brennan Manning, *Abba's Child: The Cry of the Heart for Intimate Belonging* (Colorado Springs, CO: NavPress, 2015), 40.

[9]C. S. Lewis, *Mere Christianity* (New York: Touchstone, 1996), 190.

[10]If you'd like to learn more about the daily examen, visit ignatianspirituality.com /ignatian-prayer/the-examen.

[11]Book of Common Prayer, *The Litany*, General Synod of the Anglican Church of Canada (Toronto: Prayer Book Society of Canada, 1962).

[12]*The Happy Film,* directed by Hillman Curtis, Ben Nabors, and Stefan Sagmeister (Richmond, Aus.: So So Productions LLC, 2016).

[13]SWNS, "Americans Check Their Phones 80 Times A Day: Study," New York Post, accessed March 11, 2020, https://nypost.com/2017/11/08/americans-check -their-phones-80-times-a-day-study/.

[14]Henri J. M. Nouwen, *The Return of the Prodigal Son: A Story of Homecoming* (London: Darton, Longman & Todd, 1994).

[15]Nouwen, *Return of the Prodigal Son,* 8.

[16]Nouwen, *Return of the Prodigal Son,* 137.

[17]Nouwen, *Return of the Prodigal Son,* 107.

[18]Nouwen, *Return of the Prodigal Son,* 119.

9 With—Withward in Community

[1]Dietrich Bonhoeffer, *Life Together: The Classic Exploration of Christian Community* (New York: HarperOne, 2009), 19.

[2]Bonhoeffer, *Life Together,* 20.

[3]Wesley Hill, "You Must Not Be Afraid of Looking for God in the Eyes of a Friend," Spiritual Friendship, December 14, 2015, https://spiritualfriendship.org /2015/12/14/you-must-not-be-afraid-of-looking-for-god-in-the-eyes-of-a -friend/.

[4]Bonhoeffer, *Life Together,* 27.

[5]Wesley Hill, *Spiritual Friendship: Finding Love in the Church as a Celibate Gay Christian* (Grand Rapids, MI: Brazos Press, 2015), 108.

[6]I've found Scott Peck's four stages to community to be very helpful: pseudo -community, chaos, emptiness, and true community. See M. Scott Peck, *The Different Drum* (New York: Simon and Schuster, 1987).

[7]N. T. Wright, *Simply Jesus: A New Version of Who He Was, What He Did, Why It Matters* (New York: HarperOne, 2011), 180.

[8]Kathleen Norris, *The Quotidian Mysteries* (Mahwah, NJ: Paulist Press, 1998), 1-3.

[9]C. S. Lewis, *The Four Loves* (New York: Harcourt, Inc., 1998), 71.

[10]David G. Benner, *Surrender to Love: Discovering the Heart of Christian Spirituality* (Downers Grove, IL: InterVarsity Press, 2015), 89.

[11]Wesley Hill, *Washed and Waiting: Reflections on Christian Faithfulness and Homosexuality* (Grand Rapids, MI: Zondervan, 2017), 57-58.

10 Out—Outward in Mission

[1]David Bosch, *Transforming Mission: Paradigm Shifts in Theology of Mission* (Maryknoll, NY: Orbis Books, 2011), 381.

[2]One of the reasons I like to define mission as "love on the move" is because it captures how mission existed within the Trinity prior to creation and how it will continue after the consummation of new creation. The *missio Dei* is eternal. God's love is always on the move within the Trinity and toward creation, and we join this movement now and forever.

[3]James H. Olthuis, *The Beautiful Risk: A New Psychology of Loving and Being Loved* (Grand Rapids, MI: Zondervan, 2001), 44.

[4]Lesslie Newbigin, *The Gospel in a Pluralist Society* (London: SPCK, 2014), 119.

[5]David Brooks, *The Second Mountain: How People Move from the Prison of Self to the Joy of Commitment* (New York: Random House, 2019), 122.

[6]Zack Eswine, *Sensing Jesus: Life and Ministry as a Human Being* (Wheaton, IL: Crossway, 2013), 43.

[7]James D. Bratt, *Abraham Kuyper: A Centennial Reader* (Grand Rapids, MI: Eerdmans, 1998), 488.

[8]Christine Pohl, *Making Room: Recovering Hospitality as a Christian Tradition* (Grand Rapids, MI: Eerdmans, 1999), 129.

[9]Jay Pathak and Dave Runyon, *The Art of Neighboring: Building Genuine Relationships Right Outside Your Door* (Grand Rapids, MI: Baker Books, 2012), chapter 1.

[10]Timothy Keller and Katherine Leary Alsdorf, *Every Good Endeavor: Connecting Your Work to God's Work* (New York: Penguin Books, 2016), 66.

[11]To be perfectly candid, not every neighborly relationship has gone this way. I presently live in Vancouver and know most of my neighbors. None of them have come to faith.

[12]Shaila Visser, "Alpha Is Much More than a Video Series," Church for Vancouver, September 4, 2019, https://churchforvancouver.ca/alpha-is-much-more-than-a -video-series/.

Epilogue: Godspeed

[1]Yes, this analogy breaks down if you're ambidextrous.

[2]I commend this short film to you. You can watch it for free at livegodspeed.org.

[3]Eugene H. Peterson, *A Long Obedience in the Same Direction: Discipleship in an Instant Society* (Downers Grove, IL: InterVarsity Press, 2019).

[4]This quote is from Wright's interview in *Godspeed* (livegodspeed.org).

[5]I recommend John Mark Comer's book *The Ruthless Elimination of Hurry* for anyone who struggles to slow down in life.

[6]Ken Shigematsu, *God in My Everything: How an Ancient Rhythm Helps Busy People Enjoy God* (Grand Rapids, MI: Zondervan, 2013), 27.

Appendix C: A Simple Guide to Discerning a Call to Ministry

[1]Timothy Keller and J. Allen Thompson, *Church Planter Manual* (New York: Redeemer Presbyterian Church, 2002), 65-67.

REDEEMER
CITY to CITY

Redeemer City to City is a nonprofit organization that prayerfully recruits, trains, coaches, and resources leaders who cultivate gospel movements in global cities primarily through church planting. City to City is based in New York City and works in over 140 global cities throughout Africa, Asia, Australia, North America, Latin America, the Middle East, and Europe. City to City's core competencies are urban church planting, leadership development, and content creation. All of this is done to help bring the gospel of Jesus Christ to cities.

City to City was co-founded and is chaired by Tim Keller. After transitioning out of his position as senior pastor at Redeemer Presbyterian Church, Tim Keller moved into a full-time role with City to City, focusing on ministry in global cities like Johannesburg, Mumbai, London, São Paulo, and New York City. He and City to City's global leaders work together to invest in and pass along what they have learned to a new generation of ministry leaders. Through these endeavors, City to City helps build for and propel movements of the gospel in affiliate networks around the globe.

Redeemer City to City prayerfully recruits, trains, coaches, and resources leaders to start and strengthen churches and networks in their cities. As of January 2020, City to City's global partners have planted nearly 750 churches and trained or impacted more than 40,000 leaders.

For more information visit www.redeemercitytocity.com

f RedeemerCTC

🐦 RedeemerCTC

 RedeemerCTC

▶ youtube.com/RedeemerCTC